Inspired by the Beloved Classic by
Hannah Whitall Smith

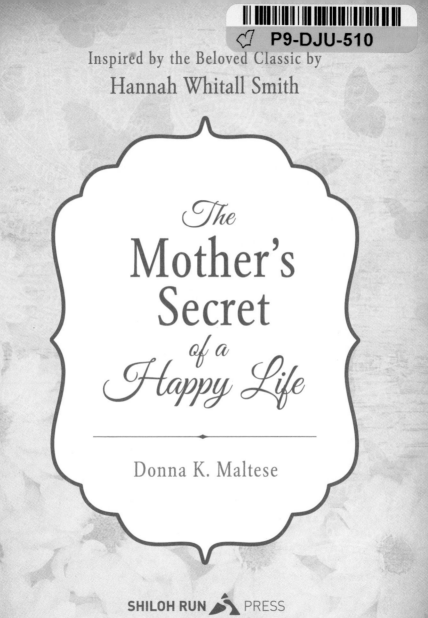

The
Mother's
Secret
of a
Happy Life

Donna K. Maltese

SHILOH RUN PRESS
An Imprint of Barbour Publishing, Inc.

© 2015 by Barbour Publishing, Inc.

Print ISBN 978-1-63058-719-2

eBook Editions:

Adobe Digital Edition (.epub) 978-1-63409-255-5

Kindle and MobiPocket Edition (.prc) 978-1-63409-256-2

Scripture quotations marked KJV are taken from the King James Version of the Bible.

Scripture quotations marked NIRV are taken from the Holy Bible, NEW INTERNATIONAL READER'S VERSION®. Copyright © 1996, 1998 Biblica. All rights reserved throughout the world. Used by permission of Biblica.

Scripture quotations marked NASB are taken from the New American Standard Bible, © 1960, 1962, 1963, 1968, 1971, 1972, 1973, 1975, 1977, 1995 by The Lockman Foundation. Used by permission.

Scripture quotations marked AMP are taken from the Amplified® Bible, © 1954, 1958, 1962, 1964, 1965, 1987 by The Lockman Foundation. Used by permission.

Scripture quotations marked NCV are taken from the New Century Version of the Bible, copyright © 2005 by Thomas Nelson, Inc. Used by permission. All rights reserved.

Scripture quotations marked CEV are from the Contemporary English Version, Copyright © 1995 by American Bible Society. Used by permission.

Scripture quotations marked TNIV are taken from the Holy Bible, Today's New International Version®. Copyright 2001, 2005 by Biblica®. Used by permission of Biblica®. All rights reserved worldwide.

Scripture quotations marked NKJV are taken from the New King James Version®. Copyright © 1982 by Thomas Nelson, Inc. Used by permission. All rights reserved.

Scripture quotations marked MSG are from *THE MESSAGE*. Copyright © by Eugene H. Peterson 1993, 1994, 1995, 1996, 2000, 2001, 2002. Used by permission of NavPress Publishing Group.

Scripture quotations marked NLT are taken from the Holy Bible, New Living Translation copyright© 1996, 2004, 2007, 2013 by Tyndale House Foundation. Used by permission of Tyndale House Publishers, Inc. Carol Stream, Illinois 60188. All rights reserved.

Scripture quotations marked GW are taken from GOD'S WORD Translation, Copyright © 1995 by God's Word to the Nations. Used by permission of Baker Publishing Group.

Scripture quotations marked TLB are taken from The Living Bible © 1971 by Tyndale House Foundation. Used by permission of Tyndale House Publishers, Inc. Wheaton, Illinois 60189. All rights reserved.

Scripture quotations marked NIV are taken from the HOLY BIBLE, NEW INTERNATIONAL VERSION®. NIV®. Copyright © 1973, 1984, 2011 by Biblica, Inc.™ Used by permission. All rights reserved worldwide.

Published by Shiloh Run Press, an imprint of Barbour Publishing, Inc., P.O. Box 719, Uhrichsville, Ohio 44683, www.shilohrunpress.com

Our mission is to publish and distribute inspirational products offering exceptional value and biblical encouragement to the masses.

Member of the
Evangelical Christian
Publishers Association

Printed in the United States of America.

Contents

*"When a woman gives birth,
she has a hard time, there's no getting
around it. But when the baby is born,
there is joy in the birth. This new life
in the world wipes out memory of
the pain. The sadness you have
right now is similar to that pain,
but the coming joy is also similar. . . .
It will be a joy no one can rob from you."*

JOHN 16:21–22 MSG

Introduction

I regard [parenting] as the hardest, most complicated,
anxiety-ridden, sweat-and-blood-producing job in the world.
Succeeding requires the ultimate in patience, common sense,
commitment, humor, tact, love, wisdom, awareness, and knowledge.
At the same time, it holds the possibility for the most rewarding,
joyous experience of a lifetime, namely, that of being successful
guides to a new and unique human being.

VIRGINIA SATIR

*A*h, motherhood—the experience that lasts a lifetime and beyond. Although
the opportunities in and around motherhood are immeasurable, it is a craft not
for the faint of heart, for it comes complete with trials and triumphs, jolts and
joys. It usually begins with moments of frustration with an infant whose sole goal
seems to be to keep you from getting any sleep—yet whose smile melts your heart.
Then there is the toddler whose propensity to climb every mountain (tables, stairs,
chairs) keeps you from ever feeling you can take a minute to relax and wishing you
actually *did* have eyes in the back of your head—yet whose every small triumph
makes you cheer as if he's just scaled Mount Everest. Before you know it, your
child is a teen, whose attitude is stretching your patience—yet whose attempts
at independence are actually helping her become the amazing adult you know
she soon will be. So how is a *mother*—defined as "a formerly somewhat sane
woman"—to keep her joy, setting an example for all the chicks in her particular
nest? By *choosing* to infuse happiness into each and every moment of every day.

According to the Bible, there are two kinds of happiness. The first is contingent
upon what is happening around us, what our circumstances are. In other words, if

things in our earthly existence are going well, we are happy.

But there is an even deeper happiness for Christians—one that is based on the calm assurance that *in spite of* what is happening around us, we are trusting in Jesus, certain that the Holy Spirit is with us and that God will work all things out for our good. It's about rising above the trials and tribulations of this life to find that unspeakable happiness, that calmness, that sweet assurance in knowing that through flood and fire, through dirty diapers and dented fenders, through curfews and crying jags, the Lord's light is upon us, shining through us, exuding a peace others are attracted to and yearn to possess.

Yes, Mom, you have the choice to be joyful or fearful, to hand your troubles over to Jesus or keep them firmly in your white-knuckled grip, to feel a growing hopelessness and desperation or feed a deep sense of peace. It is an option you choose to take each and every moment of every day, regardless of your circumstances.

This does not mean plastering a fake smile on your face while changing stinky diapers, bandaging cuts and scrapes, or babysitting colicky grandkids but rather learning to be *joy*ful instead of *woe*ful. Unlike the "worldlings" who allow their emotions to rise and fall like the stock market, we Christian mothers are to constantly abide in the deep love and joy of Christ, which are ours for the taking.

Trouble is that today's society would have us turn our focus away from joy and onto the never-ending quest to be not only wonderful mothers but also thin and beautiful Venuses, successful career women, chefs, chauffeurs, and housemaids. In this striving for worldly perfection, we can lose sight of what's *real*—the happiness of abiding in the Lord, the power of the Word, and the inspiration of the Holy Spirit.

So let's settle down to the fact that we are mothers in Christ. We are tired of being ruled by the world and are ready to embark upon a joyful journey. This does not mean we will ignore the world's myriad of woes, but we will no longer allow them to rule our state of mind or influence our sense of peace.

So take off your apron, close up your briefcase, ditch the diaper bag, slip off your sneakers, and settle into a comfortable chair. Ask God to turn your sobs to celebration, to take off your black funeral dress and clothe you with the many colors of joy (see Psalm 30:11). Open your heart, mind, soul, and spirit, and allow

The Mother's Secret of a Happy Life to help you in your quest for lasting and deep happiness.

This book was inspired by and is based in part on a classic, *The Christian's Secret to a Happy Life*, by Hannah Whitall Smith:

> *Born into a strict Quaker home in Pennsylvania in 1832, Hannah Whitall suffered from deep spiritual doubts during her early years. Her inner struggle continued into her marriage to Robert Piersall Smith in 1851, but in 1858 the couple committed their lives to Christ and decided to leave the Quaker faith to join the Plymouth Brethren.*
>
> *A further spiritual experience in 1867 led Hannah and Robert to undertake a speaking tour on the higher Christian life in the United States and Europe. As Robert's health declined, the couple stayed in England and observed the 1874 founding of the Keswick Convention, where in 1886 Amy Carmichael would feel the call of God to the mission field.*
>
> *Hannah Whitall Smith penned* The Christian's Secret of a Happy Life *in 1875 and wrote eighteen other books as well. Stricken with arthritis for the last seven years of her life and ultimately confined to a wheelchair, Smith still entertained admirers of her writings. She died in 1911.*

We hope that within the pages of *The Mother's Secret of a Happy Life*, you will find inspiration and guidance on the pathway to the joy of the Lord, tapping into Christ's amazing power and strength as you mount up with wings as eagles.

How to Use This Book

Why standest thou thus at the door? Come in, thou daughter of Abraham.
We were talking of thee but now, for tidings have come to us before,
how thou art become a pilgrim. Come, children, come in;
come, maiden, come in. So He had them all into the house.

JOHN BUNYAN, *THE PILGRIM'S PROGRESS: PART 2*

The Mother's Secret of a Happy Life can be used to find your way into the joy of the Lord each and every day. The four sections of the book cover exactly what the higher life is, the challenges along the way, the results it brings, and the new reality you experience as a "grand" mother.

To set the stage at the beginning of each chapter, you will find a quote from *The Pilgrim's Progress: Part 2*, written by John Bunyan in the late sixteen hundreds. Whereas the first part of *The Pilgrim's Progress* featured a man named Christian, the second featured the pilgrimage of his wife, Christiana, her children, and her friend Mercy. Although written centuries ago, *The Pilgrim's Progress: Part 2* is still a valid reminder of the various lessons learned by mothers journeying to Christ.

Within each chapter of *The Mother's Secret of a Happy Life*, we will also look at biblical women who follow that section's signpost—or who veer off a particular pathway, much to their detriment.

At the end of each chapter, you will find path markers relating to the material covered in that chapter. They include a key Bible promise, its proof, God's provision for its pursuit, and part of your portrait. Claim each promise, allowing the reality of its proof to sink deep. With God's provision, determine to pursue that chapter's aspect of your faith.

Part of this life-changing pursuit of happiness involves shifting not only your view of God's work in your life (and your offspring's) but the view you have of yourself (and your children). So carefully examine your personal portrait—a statement derived from a Bible passage that tells you who you truly are in Christ— and commit to memory who you are in the eyes of God.

These path markers will be followed by seven Mind-Renewing Prayers, one for each day of the week (or longer if you'd like to linger in a chapter until you believe you have truly found renewal). This will give you a chance to apply what you've learned and retrain your mind to focus on Jesus and the abundant joy found in Him instead of on the world and its life-sapping woes. God's Word tells us, "Be careful what you think, because your thoughts run your life" (Proverbs 4:23 NCV).

As you pray, read the words of each Mind-Renewing Prayer aloud and add whatever the Spirit brings to your heart. Remember that communicating with God is a two-way street. In the midst of your prayers, take the time to be still and listen for His voice.

There is no magic formula for obtaining joy. It is embedding yourself in the Word and embedding the Word in yourself—mind, body, and soul. It's trusting the One who has only the best in mind for you—regardless of how things may look, feel, or seem. It's waiting on God with hope (see Psalm 33:22).

Above all, be patient with yourself. It takes time to reconstruct and readjust your attitude to life, God, yourself, your children, and your surroundings. But never give up. God has a wonderful plan for your life as a mother and a woman. He not only is abiding with you on your inward journey but also will give you victory without.

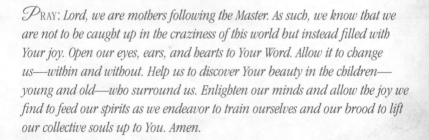

PRAY: Lord, we are mothers following the Master. As such, we know that we are not to be caught up in the craziness of this world but instead filled with Your joy. Open our eyes, ears, and hearts to Your Word. Allow it to change us—within and without. Help us to discover Your beauty in the children— young and old—who surround us. Enlighten our minds and allow the joy we find to feed our spirits as we endeavor to train ourselves and our brood to lift our collective souls up to You. Amen.

PART 1

The Life

Deep in my heart I long for your temple,
and with all that I am I sing joyful songs to you.
LORD God All-Powerful, my King and my God,
sparrows find a home near your altars;
swallows build nests there to raise their young.

PSALM 84:2–3 CEV

Chapter 1
Scripture's Stance on Joyful Deliverance

*The contents of the letter was, "That the King would have her do as did
Christian her husband; for that was the way to come to his City, and to dwell in
his presence with joy for ever." At this the good woman was quite overcome.
So she cried out to her visitor. "Sir, will you carry me and my children
with you, that we also may go and worship this King?"*
John Bunyan, *The Pilgrim's Progress: Part 2*

• • • • • • •

When we first invited Jesus into our lives, we were filled with excitement and
energy, ready to take on the world. We came to Him like little children, totally
believing that from that point on, life would be a smooth ride. We each may have
thought, *How cool is this! Nothing can stop me now! From here on out, life
will be not only* awesome—*but easy! With Jesus, I've got it made! No more
problems. No more worries.*

And then the years passed. Before we knew it, we were immersed in the
supreme testing ground—amid children who watched our every move, heard
our every word, challenged our every belief. As the months and years passed, we
watched in horror as our offspring began to mimic our words and actions. Such
an accurate reflection of ourselves gave us pause. We felt ourselves beginning to
falter. Suddenly the seemingly never-ending mountains of dirty diapers and laundry
we once felt empowered to remove began to bury us deeper and deeper. Instead of
continually tapping into Christ's power, we felt tapped out. Instead of conquering
sin, we bowed to its influence over and over again until guilt began to take hold.
We were ashamed at some of the words that came out of our mouths and burned
themselves into our children's brains. As repeat offenders in thought, word, and

deed, we doubted God's mercy, forgiveness, and overall plan. Discouraged, we distanced ourselves from the very source of light, love, peace, power, and joy that had rescued us. Like Eve in the garden, we foolishly attempted to hide from the One who sees all, from the One who could—and already did—save us.

Although we may be weary, sorrow laden, and worn, we know that hiding from God is not the answer. We must and *can* meet God face-to-face. Because of our faith in Jesus, we "can now come boldly and confidently into God's presence" (Ephesians 3:12 NLT).

It is time to realize that our lives in Christ are to be lived to the fullest, not in partial victories and agonizing defeats. We are not to live as weeping Hagars (see Genesis 21:16), slaves to sin, but as freewomen like Sarah. For once this old woman trusted God to deliver as promised, He not only brought her laughter but also made her the Mother of Nations:

> God *visited Sarah exactly as he said he would; God did to Sarah what he promised: Sarah became pregnant and gave Abraham a son in his old age, and at the very time God had set. . . . Sarah said, God has blessed me with laughter and all who get the news will laugh with me! (Genesis 21:1–2, 6 MSG)*

Once Sarah banished fear and doubt, once she stopped trying to fix things herself, once she "let go and let God," His promises—which the woman had once thought totally absurd (see Genesis 18:12)—became her reality. The result? She was overjoyed!

Are you tired of trying to do God's work in your own power? Are you willing to "let go and let God"? Are you ready to allow God's promises to become your reality? If so, you are ready to begin the quest for joyfulness!

Yet the question remains, is our joyful deliverance scriptural? Where's the proof that Jesus came to save (deliver) us? That He is all-powerful? That we are more than conquerors through Him? That because of all He has done for us, we are to be filled with joy? To find the answers, we go to the well of God's Word.

Here we find proof that Jesus did come to save us. It began with the command by an angel of the Lord who appeared to Joseph in a dream: "After her [Mary's] baby is born, name him Jesus, because he will *save* his people from their sins" (Matthew 1:21 CEV, emphasis added).

Later an angel came to the shepherds, saying, "I am bringing you good news that will be a great joy to all the people. Today your *Savior* was born in the town of David. He is Christ, the Lord" (Luke 2:10–11 NCV, emphasis added).

The amazing "birth announcements" continued, for when Mary and Joseph took their Son to the temple to offer Him to God as required by Mosaic Law, the prophet Simeon took Jesus into his arms and prayed to God, "With my own eyes I've seen your *salvation*; it's now out in the open for everyone to see" (Luke 2:30–31 MSG, emphasis added). As Simeon was praying, Anna the prophetess came on the scene, started praising God on the spot, and "talked about the child to all who were waiting expectantly for the *freeing* of Jerusalem" (Luke 2:38 MSG, emphasis added)!

After Jesus' ministry and crucifixion, others wrote of His delivering believers from death and sin (see Acts 3:26; Ephesians 4:22–24; 5:26–27; Titus 2:11–12, 14; 1 Peter 2:21–22, 24).

Hannah Whitall Smith writes, "The redemption accomplished for us by our Lord Jesus Christ on the cross at Calvary is a redemption from the power of sin as well as from its guilt. He is able to save to the uttermost all who come unto God by Him."

So, as Christians, we can have joy because we are saved—*not* because we don't sin. We still miss the mark. But we can find our joy in believing that our debt for sin has been paid in full—through the death of Jesus on the cross.

You were once dead because of your failures and your uncircumcised corrupt nature. But God made you alive with Christ when he forgave all our failures. He did this by erasing the charges that were brought against us by the written laws God had established. He took the charges away by nailing them to the cross. (Colossians 2:13–14 GW)

We rejoice because that sin, the obstacle standing between us and God, has been wiped off of us like pureed spinach off an infant's mouth. "And in addition to everything else, we" are not only free, clear, and clean of our mess, but "are happy because God sent our Lord Jesus Christ to make peace with us" (Romans 5:11 CEV).

But are we living as if we are saved and guilt-free, or are we exhausted from trying to live the holy life in our own power? Or are we hiding, hoping that no one picks up on the fact that our Christian life isn't "working"!

Here we need to believe that we—sometimes overworked and taken-for-granted moms—*have the power of the One who orchestrates the miracle of birth, takes the littlest of seeds to grow an enormous tree, and is able to quiet the sea and calm the wind*. Listen and believe Paul, who told the Ephesians, "I want you to know about the great and mighty power that God has for us followers. It is the same wonderful power he used when he raised Christ from death and let him sit at his right side in heaven" (Ephesians 1:19–20 CEV).

But how can a busy mom like you access that mighty, life-raising power? Simply let Christ live through you. Trust Him with your life. Honor Him with your mouth. Stop cowering. Stop focusing on what happened yesterday—and what may happen tomorrow. Expect Him to save you from every calamity. Be okay with not knowing the answer to every question and leaving things you don't understand up to Jesus.

Stand up straight. Let go and let God. Understand that "we are more than conquerors and gain a surpassing victory through Him Who loved us" (Romans 8:37 AMP). Know that through thick and thin, "God is on our side" (Romans 8:31 AMP), not once in a while but over and over again. Jesus "is able always to save those who come to God through him because he always lives, asking God to help them" (Hebrews 7:25 NCV).

You needn't have any fear at any time—no matter what terrors a tiny tot, testy teen, or tempestuous twenty-year-old bring to your mind! Living with God's constant courage—wow! That alone should bring joy and peace into our hearts!

So we know that in Jesus we are saved, we have access to power, and we are more than conquerors. Where then does an expectation or promise of joy come in? It comes in Christ! It comes in trusting Him, applying His Word to our lives, living out our faith.

And let's face it. There will still be earthly trials. We may lose a husband or our homes. Our children may not turn out as we had hoped. We may lose a child to sickness, drugs, or an accident. Just because we have Jesus in our lives does not mean that we won't have illness, dashed hopes, unmet expectations, and times when we just need a good cry. Jesus Himself suffered disappointment with people. He wept at the death of His friend Lazarus. But like Jesus, we can have the joy of a deep and meaningful relationship with our Abba God who has "sent forth the Spirit of His Son into our hearts, crying out, 'Abba [an Aramaic term meaning Daddy]' " (Galatians 4:6 NKJV).

But how do we get there from here? By following in Jesus' steps, walking as He walked.

Jesus wants us to have the same joy He has so that our joy will be as full as it can be (see John 15:11 NCV). All we need to do is "ask and. . .receive, so that [our] joy will be the fullest possible joy" (John 16:24 NCV). Even in the midst of kiddie crises, we can know "that these troubles produce patience" (Romans 5:3 NCV). We can remind ourselves that "in the kingdom of God"—the place where we desire to live, breathe, and serve—the truly "important things are living right with God, peace, and joy in the Holy Spirit" (Romans 14:17 NCV).

So we *can* and *should expect* joy in this life. If we don't have joy, we are not maturing in our faith. And who wants to be stunted in their growth? Paul writes to the Philippians, "I am convinced that I will remain alive so I can continue to help all of you grow and experience the joy of your faith" (Philippians 1:25 NLT). He exhorts his readers to "always be full of joy in the Lord. I say it again—rejoice!" (Philippians 4:4 NLT).

"Just as Christ was raised from the dead by the glorious power of the Father, now we also may live new lives" (Romans 6:4 NLT)—if we trust God to deliver us no matter what our circumstances. Thus, we are new mothers in Christ whether or not we feel like it. For in Him, whose presence we do not shrink from but revel in, we have available to us love, forgiveness, peace, and joy.

In Christ we—and our children—have "a friend that sticketh closer than a brother" (Proverbs 18:24 KJV), who can and will defend us against all enemies, look out for us, size up our situations, and advise us. He loves us like no other, shielding us from evil, taking on all challengers, gladly bearing our burdens. When children disappoint, well-meaning in-laws discourage, circumstances depress, or husbands desert us (physically, financially, mentally, emotionally, or spiritually), Jesus stands by our sides. He watches over us as we *and* our children sleep, guarding the gates. What joy His constant presence gives us! But we must be *aware* of His presence—within and without, above and below, to the right and the left.

Because of His sacrifice for us, we can call our Father God *Abba*! And we can be assured of the Holy Spirit's comfort and guidance.

So tell Jesus all your troubles, including sins. Tell Him you want to do better—but desperately need His help. Call on Christ's death-defying power. Count on God's protection. Follow the Holy Spirit's guidance. Sing a new song of joy unto the Lord, who sees all mothers as His dear daughters. Dance with your children in celebration of Christ's saving grace and power.

Remember that no one can take your joy away from you (see John 16:22). Refuse to be like Hagar, sitting down in the midst of your troubles, sobbing, allowing the weight of the world's woes to oppress you. Instead, open up your eyes to the wonders of God's life-changing power by following in the footsteps of Sarah, the Mother of Nations, who was once barren but then birthed laughter by "letting go and letting God."

Ask God to do the following:

> *[Open] the eyes of your understanding. . .that you may know what is the hope of His calling, what are the riches of the glory of His inheritance in the saints, and what is the exceeding greatness of His power toward us who believe, according to the working of His mighty power which He worked in Christ when He raised Him from the dead and seated Him at His right hand in the heavenly places. (Ephesians 1:18–20 NKJV)*

"When you have begun to have some faint glimpses of this power," Smith writes, "learn to look away utterly from your own weakness, and, putting your case into

His hands, trust Him to deliver you."

In the next seven days, while raising your kids, spend a few moments each day raising your happiness quotient by impressing these things in your mind as you begin your journey on the pathway to a deep, abiding joy.

"As for you, be strong and do not give up,
for your work will be rewarded."
2 CHRONICLES 15:7 TNIV

$\mathcal{P}$ATH MARKERS

$\mathcal{P}$romise

[Jesus said,] "Ask, using my name, and you will receive, and you will have abundant joy."

JOHN 16:24 NLT

$\mathcal{P}$roof

Around midnight Paul and Silas were praying and singing hymns to God, and the other prisoners were listening. Suddenly, there was a massive earthquake, and the prison was shaken to its foundations. All the doors immediately flew open, and the chains of every prisoner fell off! The jailer woke up to see the prison doors wide open. He assumed the prisoners had escaped, so he drew his sword to kill himself. But Paul shouted to him, "Stop! Don't kill yourself! We are all here!"

The jailer called for lights and ran to the dungeon and fell down trembling before Paul and Silas. Then he brought them out and asked, "Sirs, what must I do to be saved?"

They replied, "Believe in the Lord Jesus and you will be saved, along with everyone in your household." And they shared the word of the Lord with him and with all who lived in his household. Even at that hour of the night, the jailer cared for them and washed their wounds. Then he and everyone in his household were immediately baptized. He brought them into his house and set a meal before them, and he and his entire household rejoiced because they all believed in God.

ACTS 16:25–34 NLT

Provision

[Jesus said,] "I have told you these things so that you can have the same joy I have and so that your joy will be the fullest possible joy."

JOHN 15:11 NCV

Portrait

In Christ, I am able to have joy in any situation (see Philippians 4:4, 12).

MIND-RENEWING PRAYERS

DAY 1
Free Hands

Take your everyday, ordinary life—your sleeping, eating, going-to-work, and walking-around life—and place it before God as an offering. Embracing what God does for you is the best thing you can do for him.
ROMANS 12:1 MSG

Dear Lord, thank You for saving my life, for drawing me closer and closer to You. I place all that I am, all that I want to be, and all that I have—including my children—before You. Now my hands are free to accept the fact that You have delivered me from all things—including myself. I revel in that fact and rejoice in Your loving presence.

Day 2
My Children's Eyes

Don't become so well-adjusted to your culture that you fit into it without even thinking. Instead, fix your attention on God. You'll be changed from the inside out. Readily recognize what he wants from you, and quickly respond to it.
ROMANS 12:2 MSG

Jesus, help me to keep my eyes on You, not on my circumstances and not on the world around me, for all those things will one day fade away. But You, Your power, Your gift to me of eternal life, and Your Word will always be here. I am looking for You in all places, including the eyes of my children. Lead me, Lord. I am ready to follow, no questions asked.

Day 3
Suddenly Reborn

Now we look inside, and what we see is that anyone united with the Messiah gets a fresh start, is created new. The old life is gone; a new life burgeons!
2 CORINTHIANS 5:17 MSG

I'm forgetting about my past mistakes, Lord. You have given me a new life, a fresh start. Suddenly I feel reborn. In Your strength, I am re-created, allowing You to mold me into the person You want me to be, the mother You created me to be. Praise God for the chance to begin anew! May I extend as much grace to my children as You have extended to me.

Day 4

My Hope and Mainstay

*I would have lost heart, unless I had believed that I would see
the goodness of the LORD in the land of the living.*
PSALM 27:13 NKJV

*I feel as if I have been through the wringer lately, Lord. Yet there is one thing that
keeps me going, one thing I can cling to—the belief that in spite of all that has
happened, I will see Your goodness in my life. I have faith that no matter how
things look now, You, my hope and mainstay, will move in my life.*

Day 5

All That Is Good

*The fruit of the Spirit is love, joy, peace, longsuffering,
gentleness, goodness, faith, meekness, temperance.*
GALATIANS 5:22–23 KJV

*Some days are tougher than others, Jesus, but I know that when I walk in the
Spirit, I will experience all that is good, all that is God. And these gifts—love,
joy, peace, patience, compassion, kindness, belief, and self-control—will come
to fruition. May these spiritual gifts draw me closer to You and my children.*

Day 6
A Conduit of Love

Now may the God of hope fill you with all joy and peace in believing,
so that you will abound in hope by the power of the Holy Spirit.
ROMANS 15:13 NASB

Thank You so much for giving up Your life for me, for making my joy in
You a priority, a mainstay of my faith. Thank You, Abba Father. May I be a
conduit of Your love for me, allowing the joy I find in You to spill over my
children and Your peace to flow over my day.

Day 7
Witnesses

The Lord has blessed you because you
believed that he will keep his promise.
LUKE 1:45 CEV

When I put all my trust and faith in Your promises, Lord, amazing things
happen. Suddenly I have Your wisdom, Your peace. I am overflowing in Your
love. And my children feel all these things wafting off me. In that space, they
feel Your presence. And in their heart of hearts, they see You, and they, too,
become witnesses of Your promises.

CHAPTER 2
God's Side and Woman's Side

Gaius also proceeded, and said, "I will now speak on the behalf
of women, to take away their reproach. For as death and the curse came
into the world by a woman, so also did life and health: 'God sent
forth his Son made of a woman' [Galatians 4:4 KJV]."
JOHN BUNYAN, *THE PILGRIM'S PROGRESS: PART 2*

• • • • • • •

Motherhood. It all began with the first woman—Eve.

According to the creation story, God made Adam from the dust of the ground.
When God saw that man needed a suitable helper, He put Adam to sleep while He
removed a rib from his side. From that rib, God formed the first woman, whom
Adam named Eve, the Mother of All Living Things. And God called all that He had
made "very good."

Thus, the first man and woman, two perfect creatures made in the image
of God, molded directly by His hands, had the run of the Garden of Eden and full
access to their Creator. Between them and Him were no obstacles, no barriers. It
truly was paradise!

And then one day, Eve followed not God's voice but that of the serpent. She
took herself out of her Creator's hands, off His potter's wheel, and placed herself
under the influence of the evil one. Going against God's instructions, Eve ate
the forbidden fruit and prompted Adam to do the same. The result? Sin entered
the world. Man and woman's relationship with God was broken. From then on,
life would be a struggle. They would be kicked out of the Garden of Eden, Adam
would have to pick at the earth for food, and Eve would suffer tremendous pain in
childbirth. Yet God can make good out of any situation.

Edith Deen, author of *All the Women of the Bible*, writes: "Though Eve fell short of the ideal in womanhood, she rose to the dream of her destiny as a wife and mother. Paradise had been lost. . .but something wonderful, maternal care, had been born."

After suffering the anguish of childbirth, Eve gave birth to two sons—Cain and Abel. What joy and what awareness of her dependence upon the master Creator she must have felt as she held those whom God brought to life through her and Adam. Later what agony she must have experienced when she, Mother of All Living Things, lost both sons—the murderous Cain to exile and the slain Abel back to earth—in one fell swoop.

Yet in spite of Eve's shortcomings, God used her to become a bigger part of His plan. He gave her the chance to start things over. With the birth of Seth, she gained back some of the joy that had seemed to be permeate the air she had so easily breathed before the fall. With Seth, the line to Jesus—the solution to all ills brought about by disobedience to our Creator—had begun. And with the birth of Eve's grandson Enosh, the time arrived that "men began to call [upon God] by the name of the Lord" (Genesis 4:26 AMP)!

The point of the story? Since the dawn of humankind, mothers have greatly influenced each generation. It is woman who, with God's help, births children who can rise above their faults and transgressions. It is she who is the initial conduit of God's love for His little ones. It is through her caress, kiss, and gentleness that each child receives his first assurance of safety. It is in complete faith in God's goodness and hope for His plan for all lives that she tends to her helpless babe. She is her infant's first line of defense from the evils of this world—physically and spiritually. She is his initial link to the One who will ultimately shape her child's destiny. And for that little while that the child is in her care, the weight of her responsibility is palpable, borne only with the help of Jesus Christ. Through His power she begins to mold her children for Him.

At the same time we mothers are helping to shape the lives of our children, we are allowing God to shape *us* into the image of His Son, Jesus Christ. And in this shaping process, there are two definite sides—God's side and woman's side. Simply put, God's role is to reshape us and ours is to trust that He's doing it. We have already been delivered from the danger of sin brought about by Eve's temptation. Now God works to transform us, as He did Eve, from lumps of clay into vessels "unto honour, sanctified, and meet for the master's use, and prepared unto every good work" (2 Timothy 2:21 KJV).

Within this transformational journey we have aids, for God has given us the Word to follow, the power of prayer, and the assurance of His love. And as we continue on our trek, continually shaped by His transforming power, we remind ourselves and God, "O LORD, You are our Father; we are the clay, and You our potter; and all we are the work of Your hand" (Isaiah 64:8 NKJV).

In God's transformational power, we, like the first man, have been pulled up out of the miry clay pit and put into His hands. Overjoyed at our coming to Him, God begins to shift our shapes, to pull us apart, to knead us, to mold us. Our role is to remain still, patient, and pliable. Then like all potters, God puts His clay upon the wheel, spinning us, wetting us, continually turning us until He is satisfied with our new shapes and smoothes us down. We are then put into the furnace and baked until we are exactly what He envisioned us to be.

As clay, we are not expected to do the Potter's work but simply to yield ourselves up to His working. Yet in order to trust the Potter to do with us what He will, we must firmly believe in Him and the process. For as soon as we doubt and lose our focus, we begin to sink, just as Peter did when walking on the water. (See Matthew 14:27–31.)

When we lose our focus and begin to go down to the depths, it's as if we have taken ourselves out of the Potter's hands and retreated back into our clay pits. No longer surrendering ourselves to the Potter's skill, we obstruct the master Creator and so remain lumps of clay instead of blossoming into beautiful vessels.

When there is no faith, there is no trust, and no transforming work can be done. *Matthew Henry's Commentary* says that a lack of belief does, "in effect, tie [Jesus'] hands" and keeps us from becoming all He would have us be. (See Matthew 13:54–58.) God forbid we should be found wanting and remain lumps of clay. Or that we miss out on what grand plans God has in store for us because we've sunk down into the dark and deep blue sea!

May we be women and mothers who, unlike the biblical Sarah, know that nothing is too hard for God (see Genesis 18:14). Would that we would make Jesus' sweet words, "Do not be afraid; only believe" (Mark 5:36 NKJV), our moment-by-moment mantra.

Let's not dare miss the miracles He can perform, the amazing way He can transform us—who can then in turn transform the world around us, beginning with the children at our breast. How can we not trust and surrender our lives, and those of our children, to the power of Christ? How can we not put ourselves and our little ones into His capable hands and expect to become beautiful vessels, inside and out?

Hannah Whitall Smith writes:

> *All that we claim, then, in this life of sanctification is that by an act of faith we put ourselves into the hands of the Lord, for Him to work in us all the good pleasure of His will, and then, by a continuous exercise of faith, keep ourselves there. When we do it, and while we do it, we are, in the scriptural sense, truly pleasing to God, although it may require years of training and discipline to mature us into a vessel that shall be in all respects to His honor and fitted to every good work.*

We lumps of clay will not be transformed into vessels overnight. It will take many spins of the Potter's wheel. But we can rest assured that we are safer in His hands than in a deep, dark pit. And that although we may experience growing pains along with our children, we (and they) will someday be mature Christians, energized and transformed by the Holy Spirit.

In all this may we be patient, not only when it comes to our own transformation but when it comes to our children's transformation as well, regardless of their age. As Florida Scott-Maxwell said, "No matter how old a mother is, she watches her middle-aged children for signs of improvement."

So, mothers, always have hope. Continue to pray for your offspring. Keep in mind the words of Abraham Lincoln, who said, "I remember my mother's prayers and they have followed me, they have clung to me all of my life." Thus, although we may not see our children as finished vessels in our lifetime, there is always the hope that, with our prayers launched into eternity, our children will remain upon God's wheel long after we're gone.

At the same time, let's be careful not to force certain issues but love our children through all their ups and downs, realizing that we, too, suffer spiritual growing pains. Simply allow God time to work us into shapely vessels for Him and keep up our faith and belief that He is indeed doing so.

Unlike Martha, who "was worried and troubled about many things" and was "distracted with much serving," we are to follow in the footsteps of her sister, Mary, who did the "one thing. . .needed" (Luke 10:40–42 NKJV). She set herself down at Jesus' feet, listening to His every word, having "chosen that good part, which will not be taken away" (Luke 10:42 NKJV).

We need not stress ourselves out with trying to help God transform us. (Or forcing our little ones into a mold of our own making, which would merely be an attempt to take them out of God's hands—and into our own!) That's like the batter attempting to help the baker make it into a cake. It just doesn't happen. All the batter can do is keep on trusting and surrendering to its designer. Because He is molding us into what He thinks we should be and do, the stress and pressure for us to perform are removed from our lives!

Madame Jeanne Guyon writes, "It is a great truth, wonderful as it is undeniable, that all our happiness—temporal, spiritual, and eternal—consists in one thing; namely, in resigning ourselves to God, and in leaving ourselves with Him, to do with us and in us just as He pleases."

Our transformation is all part of God's process. But can we be patient in this I-want-it-now society? John Ortberg writes, "Biblically, waiting is not just something we have to do until we get what we want. Waiting is part of the process of becoming what God wants us to be."

Have you drifted out of the Potter's hands? Has impatience driven you to work in your own power or force your children onto your own potter's wheel? If so, surrender yourself and them on the altar. Put everything and everyone back into

God's hands and await His working in your lives. Allow Him to transform you all into the image of Christ "from glory to glory" (2 Corinthians 3:18 KJV).

With our Lord as our eternal master designer, with our ongoing surrender—of ourselves and our children—with our power of belief, with our patient awaiting of His working, we can be assured that God is shaping us into amazing, confident, expectant, joy-filled mothers. There's no telling what feats He is designing us to perform.

Our part is merely to trust, to surrender ourselves and our children to God's work, and to follow Christ's injunction: "Do not be seized with alarm and struck with fear; only keep on believing" (Mark 5:36 AMP). For when we truly believe, amazing things happen.

With God's help we will do mighty things.
PSALM 60:12 NLT

Path Markers
· ·

Promise

God began doing a good work in you, and I am sure he will continue it until it is finished.

PHILIPPIANS 1:6 NCV

Proof

As he went along, he saw a man blind from birth. His disciples asked him, "Rabbi, who sinned, this man or his parents, that he was born blind?"

"Neither this man nor his parents sinned," said Jesus, "but this happened so that the works of God might be displayed in him. As long as it is day, we must do the works of him who sent me. Night is coming, when no one can work. While I am in the world, I am the light of the world."

Having said this, he spit on the ground, made some mud with the saliva, and put it on the man's eyes. "Go," he told him, "wash in the Pool of Siloam" (this word means "Sent"). So the man went and washed, and came home seeing.

JOHN 9:1–7 TNIV

Provision

His divine power has given us everything we need for a godly life through our knowledge of him who called us by his own glory and goodness. Through these he has given us his very great and precious promises, so that through them you may participate in the divine nature.

2 PETER 1:3–4 TNIV

Portrait

In Christ, I am being transformed into a new person (see 2 Corinthians 5:17).

MIND-RENEWING PRAYERS

DAY 1
Miracle of Labors

Jesus answered and said to him, "Truly, truly, I say to you,
unless one is born again he cannot see the kingdom of God."
JOHN 3:3 NASB

Lord, I thank You for the physical birth of my child, although a simple "thank
You" does not seem enough for the miracle of labor. I humbly bow before
You, ever in awe of Your plan, Your ways, Your love. I thank You also for my
spiritual birth. At this very moment I put myself and my child in Your hands.
May we both be members of Your kingdom, clay upon Your wheel!

DAY 2
A Fresh Start

Create in me a clean heart, O God, and renew a right,
persevering, and steadfast spirit within me.
PSALM 51:10 AMP

I need a makeover, Lord. I'm bringing You not only my heart but also my
mind, soul, and spirit. Renew me! Allow me a fresh start in Your eyes. Give
me the strength to walk Your way and the weakness to be more pliable in Your
hands. Direct my feet, my life, my child. Help me to live You before her.

Day 3
Kingdom Residents

"Grow up. You're kingdom subjects. Now live like it.
Live out your God-created identity. Live generously and
graciously toward others, the way God lives toward you."
MATTHEW 5:48 MSG

Continually remind me, God, that I am a resident of Your kingdom. May I not bow down to anger, frustration, or sadness but to You alone and live my life the way You designed me to live—in love, patience, and joy. At the same time, my King, help me to be as merciful and gentle to my child as You are to me.

Day 4
A Family Resemblance

Each of you is now a new person. You are becoming more and
more like your Creator, and you will understand him better.
COLOSSIANS 3:10 CEV

The more I allow You to have Your way with me, Lord, the more I understand You. And the more I understand You, the more able I am to surrender myself and my child to Your care. Give me the wisdom to grow a child in Your love and light in a way that helps us both to become more and more like You so others will see a family resemblance.

DAY 5
Because of You

For I am not ashamed of the Gospel (good news) of Christ, for it is God's power working unto salvation [for deliverance from eternal death] to everyone who believes with a personal trust and a confident surrender and firm reliance.

ROMANS 1:16 AMP

You have amazing power, Lord. I could never raise this child without You. So I thank You each and every day for Your touch, Your advice, Your love. Because of You I have confidence. Because of You, I know my child will always be safe. Because of You I know all is well—in heaven and earth. Because of You, I am able to surrender all. It's all because of You.

DAY 6
Mold Me Anew

Whenever the pot the potter was working on turned out badly, as sometimes happens when you are working with clay, the potter would simply start over and use the same clay to make another pot.

JEREMIAH 18:4 MSG

I know I have failed in so many different ways. Forgive me for those short-comings, Lord. But do not allow me to sink down. Pull me up out of this pit. Mold me anew. I put myself in Your hands once again. Make me the vessel You desire me to be. And help me to allow You some room to begin molding my child. May Your will be done!

DAY 7
God's Living Children

Hosea put it well: I'll call nobodies and make them somebodies;
I'll call the unloved and make them beloved. In the place where they yelled
out, "You're nobody!" they're calling you "God's living children."
ROMANS 9:25–26 MSG

I haven't got a very good track record, Lord. I keep taking myself—and even
worse, my children—out of Your hands. As if I know better! But I know You
have better plans. You obviously are so much wiser than me. So help me to step
out of Your way. Do with me—and my child—as You will. Make us what You
always intended us to be: Your living children!

CHAPTER 3
The Life Defined

The Keeper of the gate did marvel, saying, What! is she become now a pilgrim that, but a while ago, abhorred that life. Then she [Christiana] bowed her head, and said, Yes, and so are these my sweet babes also.
JOHN BUNYAN, *THE PILGRIM'S PROGRESS: PART 2*

• • • • • • • •

*I*magine living as a Hebrew in the days of Exodus, when, by order of Egypt's pharaoh, your male baby was to be destroyed as soon as he was delivered from your womb.

One such mother was Jochebed of the house of Levi. She'd already borne Aaron and Miriam. And now, in this perilous time, she gave birth to another baby. A boy. From the beginning, this mother took the possible in hand and trusted God with the seemingly impossible. "By faith," Jochebed and her husband "hid him [Moses] for three months after he was born, because they saw he was no ordinary child, and they were not afraid of the king's edict" (Hebrews 11:23 NIV).

By faith, Jochebed then took another courageous step. When it was too dangerous to keep the child hidden from prying ears and eyes, she made a small, watertight ark from a papyrus basket, placed her beloved infant in it, and, *totally trusting God*, set it in the reeds along the bank of the crocodile-infested Nile River. Jochebed then stationed her daughter, Miriam, to watch over the basket from a distance.

The rest is a testament to what happens when a woman of faith and courage lives the life God created her to live—one of complete trust, confidence, and obedience in Him: Pharaoh's daughter rescued the child, named him Moses, and hired Jochebed to nurse him. What joy this mother must have felt to have her once-waterborne babe back in her arms. And to top it off, Moses received an amazing education among the privileged—yet, most likely due to his mother's teaching and influence, he never lost sight of the fact he was a Hebrew, one of God's chosen people. Can you imagine what this world would have lost if not for the courage and faith of Jochebed, who bore the babe who would one day see God face-to-face?

As that tiny lifeboat was to Moses, so Christ is to us—and more! In Christ we are not only saved, protected, and hidden from all perils but also assured of eternal life. This unwavering confidence in Christ is the true Christian life, best described as the "life. . .hidden with Christ in God" (Colossians 3:3 NASB). It is a higher life of continual rest in Jesus, of peace that surpasses all understanding. It's a calm assurance and abundant joy in the midst of trials and chaos.

But how do we live out this higher life? By having childlike trust and faith in God, knowing that through thick and thin, He is with us and *wants*, *asks*, *actually desires* to carry our burdens.

As mothers living in this day and age—where danger seems to lurk around every corner—we have plenty of worries to hand over to God. Perhaps we hesitate to give God our burdens because we're not sure He can handle them. How ridiculous for us to think that God—who parted the Red Sea, brought down the walls of Jericho, and made the sun stand still—cannot help us in our time of need. Or that Jesus—who calmed the wind and waves, healed the deaf, mute, blind, and lame, and rose from the dead—is unable to handle our problems.

We must train our minds and hearts to believe what the hymn writer Fanny Crosby, who was blind, understood: "I know that whate'er befall me, Jesus doeth all things well"! Notice her use of the present tense—"doeth." He is with you now, *waiting* to carry your load. To turn your trial into triumph! Will you let Him?

Perhaps we think our prayers are going nowhere, that God—too busy with bigger world problems—will not respond. That seems to be a small view of a God whose eyes are everywhere (see Proverbs 15:3). With His panoramic vision, He can see the solutions we cannot even *begin* to imagine. As J. I. Packer wrote, "There is no moment when his [God's] eye is off me, or his attention is distracted from me, no moment, therefore, when his care falters. I never go unnoticed. Every moment of life is spent in the sight and company of an omniscient, omnipresent Creator."

Not only is God constantly looking out for us, especially in our role as mothers, but He also hears and immediately responds with His all-encompassing love and affection.

After giving birth to my son Zachary, I entered the whole new world of breast-feeding. Although it is an amazing process that God in His wisdom created, it could prove to be somewhat embarrassing. Sometimes when I was away from Zach, minding my own business, I would hear a baby cry, which would immediately trigger my let-down reflex! Fortunately, I wore breast shields and had ample time to make quick exits before the dams broke.

Just as mothers immediately respond to an infant's cries, God immediately responds to our shrieks for help. Isaiah writes:

> *Zion said, "I don't get it. GOD has left me. My Master has forgotten I even exist."*
> *"Can a mother forget the infant at her breast, walk away from the baby she bore? But even if mothers forget, I'd never forget you—never."*
> *(Isaiah 49:14–15 MSG)*

Often we are so focused on our feelings, our unique temperaments, our own peccadilloes and temptations, our expectations, our own versions of what is right and wrong, our fears, and plans that we cannot see clearly. Jochebed's complete faith and trust in God freed her mind, enabling God to plant therein an amazingly creative solution to the problem of keeping her child alive. She knew where the pharaoh's daughter usually bathed. And in Jochebed's quiet confidence in God and with a prayer upon her lips, that is the sea of reeds where she launched her child's ark. Because of this positive faith, this confidence, this trust in her God, she—and her child—were rewarded above and beyond what they ever could have imagined!

Wanda E. Brunstetter writes, "Worry is the darkroom in which negatives can develop." Like Jochebed, we must not allow our worries and what-ifs to keep us in the dark or hold us in bondage. Instead, we are to abandon our entire selves to God. Yet because our old habits of worry are so deep, it may take some training to give up our self to God.

Madame Jeanne Guyon, in *Experiencing the Depths of Jesus Christ*, writes:

You must come to the Lord and there engage in giving up all your concerns. All your concerns go into the hand of God. You forget yourself, and from that moment on you think only of Him. By continuing to do this over a long period of time, your heart will remain unattached; your heart will be free and at peace!

We are to give God *all* our burdens, not only those about our children—but everything that produces those horrible worry lines. In this information age, we hear bad news from every corner of the world! It's enough to stoop our shoulders. But God reminds us over and over again that we are not to carry these burdens. We were not made for it. Nor are we to put all our focus on trouble. For when we do, we miss not only God's miracles but also His beyond-our-ken solutions!

Being constantly concerned with what may happen to our children, our home, our hearth, and ourselves limits our vision. It blinds us to the future and makes us waver in the now. If we are not focused on or looking for God's working, we find ourselves thinking up the worst-case scenarios, reasoning that we should, after all, be prepared just in case. As our thoughts careen out of control, our emotions are triggered, sinking us deeper in despair over an imagined outcome that may never be realized! Before we know it, we are caught in a whirlpool of worry! Would that we had gone to prayer before our thoughts sucked us down into the vortex.

Let's face it: It is not our circumstances that need altering. It is we ourselves. It is our mind-set that must first be shifted. Then the conditions will naturally be changed. With a simple, childlike faith in God who sees all and knows all, our whole world—indeed our entire outlook—takes on a whole new energy and perspective.

Hannah Whitall Smith gives a wonderful analogy about how to trust in God with simple faith:

Do you recollect the delicious sense of rest with which you have sometimes gone to bed at night, after a day of great exertion and weariness? How delightful was the sensation of relaxing every muscle and letting your body go in a perfect abandonment of ease and comfort! The strain of the day had ceased, for a few hours at least, and the work of the day had been laid off. You no longer had to hold up an aching head or a weary back. You trusted yourself to the bed in an absolute confidence, and it held you up, without effort, or strain, or even thought, on your part. You rested!

But suppose you had doubted the strength or the stability of your bed and had dreaded each moment to find it giving way beneath you and landing you on the floor; could you have rested then? Would not every muscle have been strained in a fruitless effort to hold yourself up, and would not the weariness have been greater than if you had not gone to bed at all?

Let this analogy teach you what it means to rest in the Lord. Let your souls lie down upon the couch of His sweet will, as your bodies lie down in their beds at night. Relax every strain, and lay off every burden. Let yourself go in a perfect abandonment of ease and comfort, sure that, since He holds you up, you are perfectly safe. Your part is simply to rest. His part is to sustain you; and He cannot fail.

Jesus Himself gives a wonderful analogy in Matthew 18:2–3, saying that unless we "become as little children," we will not be able to "enter into the kingdom of heaven" (kjv). It's likely your children don't worry about their dinner. They know that in some magical way when their playtime is over, a meal will be awaiting them. They trust you to provide whatever they need. They don't worry about tomorrow but revel in the now.

Even though you may now be a mother, you are still God's daughter, and He lovingly provides everything you *and* your children need—*in the moment*!

Trust Jesus to be your creative problem solver. Whatever your issue—yourself, your plans, your husband, your children, your work, the world's woes, your misgivings, apprehensions, or anxiety—take it to your Lord. Drop it at His feet. By faith, allow Him to take your burden upon Himself and leave you free to be and do what He has created you to be and do.

Be calm. Be carefree. Be an assured daughter of God, knowing He will never leave you. He will never forget you. He has "written your name on the palms" of His hands (see Isaiah 49:16 NIrV). He has promised to take care of you. It's not a theory but fact! Look to the lilies and the birds. If God is taking care of them, He is more than attentive to what those created in His image need, want, desire, and deal with, every moment of every day.

Like a nursing mother, when God hears your every sigh, whine, and cry, He responds immediately. You are His precious baby girl. Trust Him as you trust the earth to support you. You and your children are in His hands, heart, and thoughts. Tap into Ruth Bell Graham's wisdom: "As a mother, my job is to take care of the possible and trust God with the impossible." It is in Christ Jesus—who does all things well—that you will find your peace and rest.

> *You will keep in perfect peace all who trust in you,*
> *all whose thoughts are fixed on you!*
> ISAIAH 26:3 NLT

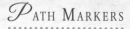

PATH MARKERS

Promise

Be careful for nothing; but in every thing by prayer and supplication with thanksgiving let your requests be made known unto God. And the peace of God, which passeth all understanding, shall keep your hearts and minds through Christ Jesus.

PHILIPPIANS 4:6–7 KJV

Proof

We do not want you to be uninformed, brothers and sisters, about the troubles we experienced in the province of Asia. We were under great pressure, far beyond our ability to endure, so that we despaired of life itself. Indeed, we felt we had received the sentence of death. But this happened that we might not rely on ourselves but on God, who raises the dead. He has delivered us from such a deadly peril, and he will deliver us again. On him we have set our hope that he will continue to deliver us.

2 CORINTHIANS 1:8–10 TNIV

Provision

"But seek first His kingdom and His righteousness, and all these things will be added to you."

MATTHEW 6:33 NASB

Portrait

In Christ, I know God will provide me with everything I need (see Philippians 4:19).

MIND-RENEWING PRAYERS

DAY 1
Now I Stand

If you are tired from carrying heavy burdens,
come to me and I will give you rest.
MATTHEW 11:28 CEV

Lord, I feel so stooped over. So trapped in my own worries and what-ifs—
about the kids, my work, my world. It's exhausting. You did not create me to
carry such a load. So I come to You today, bringing all my woes. One by one,
I name them and leave them at Your feet. And now I stand in Your presence,
lighter and at peace.

DAY 2
Be My Ark

Do not let your hearts be troubled, neither let them be afraid.
[Stop allowing yourselves to be agitated and disturbed; and do not permit
yourselves to be fearful and intimidated and cowardly and unsettled.]
JOHN 14:27 AMP

Lord, the problems I gave You yesterday are creeping back into my mind
today. I feel paralyzed by fear. My heart is heavy. I don't want to live in the
world of anxiety but in the light of Your love. Help me to have the faith of
Jochebed. Steady calm in the midst of heartbreak is what I desire. Jesus,
be my ark. Keep me riding above the waves.

Day 3
Every Breath I Take

*"Give your entire attention to what God is doing right now,
and don't get worked up about what may or may not happen tomorrow.
God will help you deal with whatever hard things come up when the time comes."*
MATTHEW 6:34 MSG

*I'm resting in the now, Jesus. I am keeping my eyes on You and You alone.
I'm taking things one day, one hour, one moment at a time. I am hiding
in Your love. Keep me close to You. Do not allow me to slip away from Your
presence. With every breath I take, even in the midst of children clamoring for
my attention, I remain in You.*

Day 4
Five Simple Words

*Jesus heard what they said, and he said to Jairus,
"Don't worry. Just have faith!"*
MARK 5:36 CEV

*Those five words seem so simple. Burn them on my brain, Lord, so they are
easily accessed in times of need. May I revel in Your calm—untouched by
calamity, unreachable by strife, unburdened by trouble. I pray that as I allow
Your perfect peace to flow over me, an ample amount spills over my children,
giving them a foretaste of You.*

DAY 5
Heaven on Earth

"I tell you the truth, you must accept the kingdom of
God as if you were a little child, or you will never enter it."
MARK 10:15 NCV

There are so many things our children can teach us. One of them is how to trust unwaveringly in You. Remove all my doubts, Lord. Reassure me with Your Word. Ease my burdens. Bring back to me the innocence and faith I had as a child. Show me the path that leads to Your kingdom—my heaven on earth.

DAY 6
Still My Father

You are God's child, and God will give you the
blessing he promised, because you are his child.
GALATIANS 4:7 NCV

Whew, Lord. What a relief to know that no matter how old I am or how gray I get, You are still my Father. You will never leave nor forsake me. You are always looking for ways to bless me. Help me to keep my focus on You. Take my hand. Never let me go.

DAY 7

Continual Peace

*Now may the Lord of peace Himself continually
grant you peace in every circumstance.*
2 THESSALONIANS 3:16 NASB

*Jesus, You know me inside out. Your eyes are always upon me. You respond
to my every cry. You know my issues, shortcomings, and sometimes-wavering
faith. Take charge of me, Lord. Help me in each and every situation. Remind
me of Your presence. Imbue me with Your peace—no matter what is
happening in my world.*

CHAPTER 4
How to Enter In

[Christiana and her friend Mercy] had no sooner got over [the Slough of Despond], but they thought they heard words that said unto them, "Blessed is she that believes; for there shall be a performance of those things that have been told her from the Lord" [Luke 1:45].

JOHN BUNYAN, *THE PILGRIM'S PROGRESS: PART 2*

· · · · · · ·

To enter into this Christian life, there is something we must understand: this life in Christ is not something we can earn. We can do nothing but ask for it—and receive this gift from God—by faith.

Naaman, an Old Testament general of the army of Aram, was a leper. A young Israeli girl he had captured was a maid to Naaman's wife. One day this servant recommended Naaman go to Samaria, knowing Elisha, the prophet there, could heal the general's skin.

So Naaman went with his horses and chariots and waited at the door of Elisha's house. But Elisha sent a messenger out to him with this message: "Go and wash yourself seven times in the Jordan River. Then your skin will be restored, and you will be healed of your leprosy." (2 Kings 5:9–10 NLT)

But Naaman refused Elisha's remedy! To this proud general, the prophet's advice made no sense. If dipping himself in a river would have cured Naaman, he could've done that back in Damascus. Fortunately, his servants talked him into following Elisha's advice. The result? Naaman put himself entirely in Elisha's hands and was immediately cured!

That is the same way we must surrender our lives to God. We must put ourselves entirely in His hands and allow Him to have His way with us—no matter how we feel or what we judge to be right or ridiculous! Doing so will inevitably lead to a life of blessings and peace in Christ, for Father God wants only what is best for us.

Yet some of us are afraid of giving ourselves totally to God. We believe He will endeavor to make our lives miserable, that He will take away all the things we love and enjoy, that all our perceived blessings will fall by the wayside. But that is not in accordance with God's Word:

> *"Suppose your son asks for bread. Which of you will give him a stone? Or suppose he asks for a fish. Which of you will give him a snake? Even though you are evil, you know how to give good gifts to your children. How much more will your Father who is in heaven give good gifts to those who ask him!" (Matthew 7:9–11 NIrV)*

Can you imagine what Mary, the mother of Jesus, would have missed had she not been totally surrendered to God, certain that He had only the best in mind for her and her child? Let's take a look at Mary. Here is this girl, engaged to a carpenter named Joseph. Then one day, Gabriel, an angel of God, makes a surprise visit. "Greetings, favored woman! The Lord is with you!" (Luke 1:28 NLT).

So far, so good. Who wouldn't want to hear a greeting like that? Of course, the angel's entrance must've been pretty scary, for Gabriel told her not to be afraid. Then he laid out God's amazing plan, His cure for the world's woes—Jesus. "The power of the Most High God will cover you. So the holy one that is born will be called the Son of God" (Luke 1:35 NIrV). And in case she had any doubts about God's ability to do anything that needed doing, Gabriel told her that her older relative, Elizabeth, was six months pregnant. "For with God nothing is ever impossible and no word from God shall be without power or impossible of fulfillment" (Luke 1:37 AMP).

Mary responded to all this shocking news with two amazing sentences: "I serve the Lord," and "May it happen to me just as you said it would" (Luke 1:38 NIrV).

Afterward, Mary went off to visit Elizabeth, whose yet-to-be-born baby, upon hearing Mary's voice, jumped for joy in Elizabeth's womb, prompting Elizabeth to say, "You are a woman God has blessed. You have believed that what the Lord has said to you will be done!" (Luke 1:45 NIrV).

Mary was so joyous that she sang a humble song about all the Lord had done for His people and how He had taken special notice of Mary herself.

With every step of the journey for herself and her Son, Mary continually relinquished herself and her Son to God—before, during, and after the birth of her precious baby who must've lit up her world like no other baby ever would (or could) again. She pondered the announcements of visiting shepherds and the pronouncements of prophets Simeon and Anna at the temple. In all things she faced—from the first visit of Gabriel to the last appearance of her resurrected Son—she remained blessed, for she never doubted her God, never wavered from His plan, never abandoned her duty.

Now ladies, is it not true that God Himself is much more loving to us than we could ever be to one cherished individual—even our own child? Isn't He the One who, through Mother Mary, gave us His one and only Son to save us from our sins? To save us from ourselves? Is it not true that He is just aching for us to enter not only the kingdom of God but the kingdom of heaven? Smith writes:

> *Heaven is a place of infinite bliss because His will is perfectly done there, and our lives share in this bliss just in proportion as His will is perfectly done in them. He loves us—loves us, I say—and the will of love is always blessings for its loved one. Could we but for one moment get a glimpse into the mighty depths of His love, and our hearts would spring out to meet His will and embrace it as our richest treasure; and we would abandon ourselves to it with an enthusiasm of gratitude and joy that such a wondrous privilege could be ours.*

Our words to our loving God must be, "Thy will be done," or as Mary said, "May it happen to me just as you said it would" (Luke 1:38 NIrV). In order to say that, we must have faith—an essential element necessary to receive any gift. For nothing—especially that which is purely mental or spiritual—ever really becomes ours until we *believe* it has been given wholeheartedly and then *claim* it as our own precious gift.

Remember how much Christ loves us and how we cannot be separated from that love? Remember how much He has forgiven us? Unless we believe in this love and forgiveness and claim both as our own, they are not really ours. Yet when it comes to living our lives for Christ, we lose sight of these principles and think that once we're saved and forgiven, we need to live by works and effort. Instead of *receiving* all He has to offer, we begin *doing*, trying to work our way into the kingdom when in actuality we have already arrived!

It's a matter of moving from "then" into "now."

Then you were "disobedient to God," but *now* you have "obtained mercy" (Romans 11:30 NKJV). *Then* "you therefore have received Christ Jesus the Lord" in faith. *Now* "walk in Him" by faith (Colossians 2:6 NKJV). *Then* "Christ Jesus has set you free from the law of sin and death" (Romans 8:2 NASB). *Now* "do not walk according to the flesh but according to the Spirit" (Romans 8:4 NASB). *Then* "the Son makes you free" from the bondage of sin; *now* "be free indeed" (John 8:36 NASB). *Then* you were "striving to please men" (Galatians 1:10 NASB). *Now* seek to please "God who examines our hearts" (1 Thessalonians 2:4 NASB). *Then* Christ lifted you "up also out of an horrible pit" (Psalm 40:2 KJV), but *now* you are set "down in highest heaven in company with Jesus" (Ephesians 2:6 MSG). *Then* "by grace you have been saved through faith, and that not of yourselves; it is the gift of God" (Ephesians 2:8 NKJV); *now* "according to your faith let it be to you" (Matthew 9:29 NKJV). *Then* "you were once darkness," but *now* "you are light in the Lord. Walk as children of light" (Ephesians 5:8 NKJV).

Are we getting the picture? Are we living in the shadows of "then" or the light of "now"? Mothers in Christ, how we will live in Christ is "according to our faith." That has always been the limit and the rule. And this faith must be a present—*now*—faith.

Smith writes, "No faith that looks for a future deliverance from the power of sin will ever lead a soul into the life we are describing. Perhaps no four words in the language have more meaning in them than the following": *Jesus saves me now.* Repeat these words over and over again—not only with your voice but with your heart, with your soul, and with your spirit. Each time emphasize a different word:

> *Jesus* saves me now. (It is *He* who continually saves you.)
> Jesus *saves* me now. (It is His *work*, not yours, *to save you continually*.)
> Jesus saves *me* now. (*You are the one* He is continually saving.)
> Jesus saves me *now*. (He is saving you *every moment of every day*—right now!)

The more time we spend in Christ, the more we remind ourselves of His gift of saving power, the more we become like Him and the closer we grow to God.

> *By his divine power, God has given us everything we need for living a godly life. We have received all of this by coming to know him, the one who called us to himself by means of his marvelous glory and excellence. And because of his glory and excellence, he has given us great and precious promises. These are the promises that enable you to share his divine nature and escape the world's corruption caused by human desires. (2 Peter 1:3–4 NLT)*

How wonderful is that taste of heaven, that divine nature that becomes part of us as we remain hidden in Christ. To enter into this blessed new life of interior rest and triumph, we take two steps—entire abandonment and absolute faith. When we endeavor to focus on those two things, we will reach that higher life far sooner than we ever imagined possible at this very moment!

John Greenleaf Whittier writes, "The steps of faith fall on the seeming void, but find the rock beneath." Christ is a mighty rock on which we stand in this life and the next. So don't be afraid to take these steps of faith, knowing that:

> *God can do anything, you know—far more than you could ever imagine or guess or request in your wildest dreams! He does it not by*

pushing us around but by working within us, his Spirit deeply and gently within us. (Ephesians 3:20 MSG)

Learn from Mary, the most magnificent example of motherhood. May we be as blessed as this woman who had no doubt that *once one enters into the spiritual life, there is a glorious love much more powerful, transcendent, and all-encompassing than that of any human family bond.* Follow in the footsteps of the woman who knew that with God's help, a mother can endure those things she cannot change.

Through it all, keep in mind that God, who calls you to enter the land of milk and honey, has given you all the courage you need to reach that Promised Land. For He has given you Himself.

I will be with thee: I will not fail thee, nor forsake thee. Be strong and of a good courage. . . . Only be thou strong and very courageous. . . . Have not I commanded thee? Be strong and of a good courage; be not afraid, neither be thou dismayed: for the Lord thy God is with thee whithersoever thou goest. . . . Only be strong and of a good courage.
JOSHUA 1:5–7, 9, 18 KJV

PATH MARKERS

Promise

"It shall be done to you according to your faith."

MATTHEW 9:29 NASB

Proof

As Jesus passed on from there, two blind men followed Him, shouting loudly, Have pity and mercy on us, Son of David!

When He reached the house and went in, the blind men came to Him, and Jesus said to them, Do you believe that I am able to do this? They said to Him, Yes, Lord.

Then He touched their eyes, saying, According to your faith and trust and reliance [on the power invested in Me] be it done to you; and their eyes were opened.

MATTHEW 9:27–30 AMP

Provision

For God, who said, "Light shall shine out of darkness," is the One who has shone in our hearts to give the Light of the knowledge of the glory of God in the face of Christ.

2 CORINTHIANS 4:6 NASB

Portrait

In Christ, I am standing firm (see 1 Thessalonians 3:8).

MIND-RENEWING PRAYERS

DAY 1

Moving Ahead in the Light

Open my eyes so I can see what you
show me of your miracle-wonders.
PSALM 119:18 MSG

Lord, give me the faith and commitment, endurance and joy, love and light
that Mary, mother of Jesus, had. Help me to enter into the life that is lived not
cowering in the shadows of fear, but moving boldly ahead in the light. Make
me a mother who finds joy and hope in all You have to offer.

DAY 2

Your Plans

Roll your works upon the Lord [commit and trust them wholly to Him;
He will cause your thoughts to become agreeable to His will,
and] so shall your plans be established and succeed.
PROVERBS 16:3 AMP

I have these worries careening around in my head. Anxiety seems to have taken
over. But none of this is of You, Lord. Take all these problems out of my hands,
for I no longer want to hold them. Fill my head with Your thoughts, my hand
with Your hand, my mouth with Your words. Make Your plans my plans.

DAY 3
The Wherewithal

I will not be afraid, because the LORD is with me.
People can't do anything to me.
PSALM 118:6 NCV

Nothing can touch me when I am abiding in You, God. You are the rock that is higher than I. You are the shield, fortress, and mighty power that saves me from everything and everyone—including myself. Here I find the courage to be the mother You have created me to be. Here I hit upon the wherewithal to do what You have called me to do.

DAY 4
In Your Heart of Hearts

Nothing now, nothing in the future, no powers, nothing above us,
nothing below us, nor anything else in the whole world will ever be
able to separate us from the love of God that is in Christ Jesus our Lord.
ROMANS 8:38–39 NCV

I am amazed at the fathomless depths and immeasurable heights Your love can reach. I am astounded that You love me, even when I feel so unlovable. And I am grateful You've made me a woman, given me a child, and promised to keep both of us in Your heart of hearts—inseparable from now through eternity.

Day 5
Forever Yours

[God] did not spare his own Son but gave him for us all.
So with Jesus, God will surely give us all things.
ROMANS 8:32 NCV

There are no words that can express how grateful I am that You gave up Your precious Son, Jesus, to heal the breach, to bring me and my child(ren) back to You. May we rest easy knowing that a God who has made such a sacrifice is One in whom we know we are forever safe, forever loved, forever Yours.

Day 6
Safe in Your Arms

Then you will go safely on your way, and you will not hurt your foot.
When you lie down, you will not be afraid. As you lie there,
your sleep will be sweet. Do not be afraid. . . . The LORD will be
your confidence. He will keep your foot from getting caught.
PROVERBS 3:23–26 GW

Lord, some nights I lie in bed, thinking of all the dangers this world poses. I wander to my child's bedroom door, unsettled until I hear her breath, long, even, precious. I stumble back to bed, wishing for a good night's rest. And then I remember, You are watching over us. You are my confidence. Soon I drift off, safe in Your arms.

DAY 7

Beam Me Up

The Lord is good, a Strength and Stronghold in the day of trouble;
He knows (recognizes, has knowledge of, and understands)
those who take refuge and trust in Him.

NAHUM 1:7 AMP

You know my weakness, God. You know how easily I can be shaken. Help me
not to lose heart. Remind me of Your stronghold. Lead me to Your fortress.
Beam me up to a broad place where no one can touch me, where I have plenty
of room to stand tall, gain strength, find courage, see You—the One who
always understands.

PART 2:

Challenges

Are not five sparrows sold for two pennies?
And [yet] not one of them is forgotten or uncared for in
the presence of God. But [even] the very hairs of your
head are all numbered. Do not be struck with fear
or seized with alarm; you are of greater worth
than many [flocks] of sparrows.

LUKE 12:6–7 AMP

CHAPTER 5

Challenges concerning Dedication

*When we came at the Hill Difficulty, [Mr. Fearing] made no stick at that,
nor did he much fear the lions; for you must know that his trouble was
not about such things as those; his fear was about his acceptance at last.*
JOHN BUNYAN, *THE PILGRIM'S PROGRESS: PART 2*

• • • • • • • •

*J*ust as the Holy Spirit awakens our soul, which then begins its upward journey
of a higher life in Christ, just when we begin to hunger and thirst for Jesus, to do
right and to *be* right with God, myriad challenges begin to face us.

The main initial challenge concerns our consecration or dedication. Smith
writes:

> *The seeker after holiness is told that he must consecrate himself, and he
> endeavors to do so. But at once he meets with a difficulty. He has done it as
> he thinks, and yet he finds no difference in his experience; nothing seems
> changed as he has been led to expect it would be, and he is completely
> baffled and asks the question almost despairingly, "How am I to know
> when I am consecrated?"*

Here we find the temptation to follow our feelings instead of our God. When we base
the truth of God and our commitment to Him or our holiness on what we feel—or
don't feel—we are misdirected, thinking that perhaps we have not given ourselves
over to or truly dedicated ourselves to God at all.

Since our feelings contradict the truth—that we have indeed committed
heart, body, mind, and soul over to God—we begin to believe we have somehow

found our way out of His hands, when the truth of the matter is that once in His hands, we can never be plucked out (see John 10:28). Smith writes, "As usual, we put feeling first and faith second, and fact last of all. Now, God's invariable rule in everything is, fact first, faith second, and feelings last of all."

To meet the challenge of our dedication to God, we need to get in line with His order of things—fact, faith, and only then feeling. So be courageous. After turning yourself—heart, mind, body, and soul—entirely over to God, consider it a fact that you are His to do with as He will. He has accepted you—lock, stock, and barrel. Allow your faith to kick in. Know that you are in His hands, that He will work through You to do His will. As the days go by, don't give in to the idea that nothing has really changed just because you don't *feel* it. This kind of wrestling will go on and on unless you cut it short by faith. Smith writes, "Come to the point of considering that matter an accomplished and settled thing, and leave it there before you can possibly expect any change of feeling whatever."

In the beginning of 1 Samuel 1, we read of Hannah, wife number one of Elkanah. Wife number two was Peninnah. Like Rachel and Leah, respectively, Hannah was barren and Peninnah was not.

To really understand this story, we must remember that in Old Testament days, a childless woman was looked upon as not living out her life purpose. So here we have barren Hannah being taunted by wife number two. On top of that, although Hannah was Elkanah's favorite, he didn't understand why she wasn't happy. After all, he asked, "Am I not of more worth to you than ten sons?" (1 Samuel 1:8 MSG).

Inconsolable, Hannah did what a truly dedicated woman of God would do: the tearful Hannah took her petition, her feelings, and her entire self—mind, body, spirit, and soul—and poured her heart out to the Lord in prayer. She said: "LORD, you rule over all. Please see how I'm suffering! Show concern for me! Don't forget about me! Please give me a son! If you do, I'll give him back to you. Then he will serve you all the days of his life" (1 Samuel 1:11 NIrV). After her prayer, she got up and had something to eat, and her face was no longer sad. That's because she "came to herself" (see Luke 15:17 KJV) and reprioritized. She put fact first, faith second, and feelings (now in God's hands) last of all. About Hannah, Matthew Henry writes:

She had by prayer committed her case to God and left it with him, and now she was no more perplexed about it. She had prayed for herself, and Eli had prayed for her, and she believed that God would either give her the mercy she had prayed for or make up the want of it to her some other way.

Unlike the once-barren women (Sarah and Rachel) who preceded her, Hannah did not take matters into her own hands, and neither did she demand her husband give her children. She merely put her entire situation and feelings—even her unborn child—into God's hands. And scripture tells us that God did indeed answer Hannah's prayer.

After her son Samuel was born, Hannah kept her promise and dedicated him to God, leaving him, once weaned, to serve at the temple. She was, in effect, merely giving God what she'd asked for and already received from Him (see 1 Chronicles 29:14, 16). Then she sang a song to the Lord, in which she focused on the Giver, not the gift, and rejoiced in the Lord, not her son (see 1 Samuel 2:1–10). The result? "The Lord was gracious to Hannah. She [again] became pregnant. Over a period of years she had three more sons and two daughters. During that whole time the boy Samuel grew up serving the Lord" (1 Samuel 2:21 NIrV).

How commendable that this woman of faith took all her grief and shame to the Lord, turned *everything* over to Him, knowing that He was her only hope, her only remedy, who held her only answer.

Are you afraid to turn yourself over *completely* to God? Afraid of pouring out your heart, telling Him your deepest dreams and desires? Afraid of losing your "self," which you have grown fond of over the years? You need not be!

In C. S. Lewis's *The Screwtape Letters*, a senior devil writes to his minion:

When He [Jesus, their "Enemy"] talks of their losing their selves, He means only abandoning the clamour of self-will; once they have done that, He really gives them back all their personality, and boasts (I am afraid, sincerely) that when they are wholly His they will be more themselves than ever.

Under Levitical law, everything given to God, because it had been given, became something holy, or consecrated (see Leviticus 27:28). It had been set apart. And although we are no longer under Levitical law, there is still a parallel. Romans 12:1 implores Christians "to give your bodies to God because of all he has done for you. Let them be a living and holy sacrifice—the kind he will find acceptable. This is truly the way to worship him" (NLT). So, having given ourselves to the Lord, we are now *holy*—and wholly His—whether we *feel* like it or not!

Another challenge linked to your feelings is your behavior. It's a known fact that your thoughts fuel your feelings, and your feelings orchestrate your actions (see Proverbs 23:7 KJV). So if you do not feel totally dedicated to God, you will certainly not act like it. This will force you to try to *act* holy on the surface, trying in your own power to do all the things a saintly mother should do—keeping a stiff upper lip, plastering a smile on your face, biting your tongue. *And* wearing all the masks you think you should be wearing—chauffeur, nursery worker, Sunday school teacher, soccer coach, homeroom volunteer, playground attendant, and member of the parent-teacher organization. In the process of going through the motions and keeping up all the facades, you end up wearing yourself out!

God has made you a new woman in Christ (see Colossians 3:10)! You have been designed to be what *He* wants you to be! And through the power of the Holy Spirit, God has given you the same power and strength as Christ, to be that new woman—one who knows God has the best in mind for her. That her Father is the One this mother can run to.

Being a saint, being *consecrated*, isn't based on our feelings or behavior. It's based on the power God has given us as we have fully committed ourselves to Him. He will work through us, to help us walk as Christ did, if we just believe. For that we need prayer and faith.

To make our prayers more effective, we need to believe God is real—even though He is not visible to our human eyes. We must believe that His presence is a certain thing and that He sees everything we do and hears everything we say. Smith writes, "Then we shall cease to have such vague conceptions of our relations with Him and shall feel the binding force of every word we say in His presence." This takes the faith described in Hebrews 11:1—"the substance of things hoped for, the evidence of things not seen" (KJV).

If you are not sure you've committed yourself wholeheartedly to God, do so now. Imagine God beside you. Pray, "Dear Lord, in this moment, and for all the moments to come, I turn myself—mind, body, heart, and soul—over to You. May Your will be done in my life. And may I have only one mask to wear—that of Your daughter."

"Your emotions may clamor against the surrender," Smith writes, "but your will must hold firm. It is your purpose God looks at, not your feelings about that purpose."

You are now in His hands, ready to receive and *use* the power and strength of the Holy Spirit to do what God wills you to do, to be who He wants you to be. If you begin to doubt your surrender, your wavering faith will cause both you and your experience to be wave- and wind-tossed. So take the remedy of repeating over and over, "Lord, I am Your daughter—heart, mind, body, and soul. I give myself entirely to You. I believe You have accepted me, and I put myself entirely in Your hands. Work through me to be the woman and mother You have called me to be. I trust You now and forevermore."

Through the power and guidance of the Holy Spirit, may this be your moment-by-moment prayer as a daughter of God and a mother of men. Make it a continual practice to abide in Christ. Consider it a fact that you are a saint indeed, holy, wholly His, and pleasing in God's sight. And that it is God, and God alone, who makes you truly happy. For when you dedicate your entire self to Him, you are only giving back what was once already His.

Hannah prayed: You make me strong and happy, LORD.
You rescued me. Now I can be glad.
1 SAMUEL 2:1 CEV

$\mathcal{P}$ATH MARKERS

$\mathcal{P}$romise

"Nothing that a man irrevocably devotes to GOD from what belongs to him. . . may be either sold or bought back. Everything devoted is holy to the highest degree; it's GOD's inalienable property."

LEVITICUS 27:28 MSG

$\mathcal{P}$roof

"Who am I, and who are these my people, that we should presume to be giving something to you? Everything comes from you; all we're doing is giving back what we've been given from your generous hand. As far as you're concerned, we're homeless, shiftless wanderers like our ancestors, our lives mere shadows, hardly anything to us. GOD, our God, all these materials—these piles of stuff for building a house of worship for you, honoring your Holy Name—it all came from you! It was all yours in the first place! I know, dear God, that you care nothing for the surface—you want us, our true selves—and so I have given from the heart, honestly and happily. And now see all these people doing the same, giving freely, willingly—what a joy!"

1 CHRONICLES 29:14–17 MSG

$\mathcal{P}$rovision

[Jesus] has reconciled you to himself through the death of Christ in his physical body. As a result, he has brought you into his own presence, and you are holy and blameless as you stand before him without a single fault.

COLOSSIANS 1:22 NLT

Portrait

In Christ, I am holy, pure in God's sight, and empowered by the Holy Spirit (see Ephesians 1:4).

Mind-Renewing Prayers

Day 1

Standing in the Truth

You are holy. . . . But you must continue to believe this truth and stand firmly in it. Don't drift away from the assurance you received when you heard the Good News.
Colossians 1:22–23 nlt

Lord, sometimes when I take my entire self into my own hands, I lose sight of You very quickly. I begin trying to do things in my own power. That's usually when I fall flat on my face—in front of my children and others. So I bring myself to You today, asking Your help in making me strong, in building up my faith. Help me stand firm in Your truth.

DAY 2
Fallen Short

*Doing whatever you feel like whenever you feel like it,
and grabbing whatever attracts your fancy. That's a
life shaped by things and feelings instead of by God.*
COLOSSIANS 3:5 MSG

*My feelings have led me astray once again, Lord. Why do I keep allowing
the idea to prevail that You are distant, that You cannot reach me—
when scripture tells me that "God's arm is not amputated—he can
still save" (Isaiah 59:1 MSG)? It's not You, Lord—it's I who have fallen short.
Forgive me. For here I come, turning my entire self over to You.*

DAY 3
A Myriad of Blessings

*You were consecrated (set apart, hallowed), and you were
justified [pronounced righteous, by trusting] in the name of
the Lord Jesus Christ and in the [Holy] Spirit of our God.*
1 CORINTHIANS 6:11 AMP

*Lord, I know You have set me apart for a special purpose, part of which is
being a mother. I also know that everything I am and have—including my
children—was Yours from the very beginning. I thank You for "loaning" me
my kids. Such a gift brings a myriad of blessings I never can repay. Lord,
make me worthy of all I've received.*

Day 4
People of Your Kingdom

*I also pray that you will understand the incredible greatness of
God's power for us who believe him. This is the same mighty power
that raised Christ from the dead and seated him in the place
of honor at God's right hand in the heavenly realms.*
EPHESIANS 1:19–20 NLT

Your resurrection power, God, is what helps me be the woman You've made
me to be. Your strength is what keeps me sane as a mother. And Your love is
the ribbon on top of the gift that is You. Thank You for creating me—and my
children. Help me to grow them into people of Your kingdom—mind, body,
spirit, and soul.

Day 5
The True Joy

*I pray that your hearts will be flooded with light so that you can
understand the confident hope he has given to those he called—
his holy people who are his rich and glorious inheritance.*
EPHESIANS 1:18 NLT

Earthly wealth is nothing compared to the riches of Your presence, God. Thank
You for allowing me to pour my heart out to You. For allowing Your Son to
pay for my wrongdoings. For being the true joy in and light of my life. For
giving me the knowledge that You will never grow tired of me, no matter how
many burdens I leave at Your feet.

DAY 6
Back to You

*"And now I entrust you to God and the message of his
grace that is able to build you up and give you an
inheritance with all those he has set apart for himself."*

ACTS 20:32 NLT

When I am down, God, You build me up. When I can no longer walk, You
carry me. When I am filled with tears, You take on the burdens of my heart.
When I am weary of the world's woes, You give me hope. May all these things I
treasure in You be what my children inherit when they give their hearts back
to You.

DAY 7
I Am Yours

*The grace (blessing and favor) of the Lord Jesus Christ (the Messiah)
be with all the saints (God's holy people, those set apart for God,
to be, as it were, exclusively His). Amen (so let it be)!*

REVELATION 22:21 AMP

I am Yours only. Thank God! Because I cannot live this life alone. Thank You
for Your many blessings, Your untiring ear, Your persistent patience, Your
hand that holds all my tears. May all that I am always be Yours—and may
this be a fact of faith I remember every moment of every day.

CHAPTER 6
Challenges concerning Faith

*Then, said He [The Interpreter or Holy Spirit],
be not afraid, only believe, and speak thy mind.*
JOHN BUNYAN, *THE PILGRIM'S PROGRESS: PART 2*

· · · · · · ·

Other possible potholes in the soul's pathway to the joy of a higher life in Christ are challenges relating to a mother's faith.

At our first baby steps in this Christian life, we may have imagined faith would be something we could feel, such as a heart overwhelmed with belief in God when we've received an answer to prayer or an unexpected blessing. As mothers, we all must have, at some point, nursed a child who had a high temperature. When the fever is raging, we make a fervent prayer to God, asking Him to please lay His hand upon our child. This, more often than not, results in that all-encompassing relief we feel when the child's fever comes down, prompting us to say to ourselves, *Now that is* faith *that I feel deep within*.

Or we might just have surface faith—the faith we think we can use to purchase God's blessings: *I have faith, so I will get what I want*.

Yet most times, faith is something that keeps us looking to the Lord during times of trial, knowing that we can trust the One who knows so much better than we do that no matter what the result, we have God on our side—the most faithful, reliable, always-there-when-we-need-Him companion of mothers. This is the kind of faith we cannot see, touch, taste, hear, or smell. It's also the kind of faith that keeps us worshipping God, regardless of the answers He may give us. Smith gives her own definition of *faith*:

[Faith] is simply believing God. You see something and thus know that you have sight; you believe something and thus know that you have faith. For as sight is only seeing, so faith is only believing. If you believe the truth, you are saved; if you believe a lie, you are lost. Your salvation comes, not because your faith saves you, but because it links you to the Savior who saves.

Faith, then, is simply believing God when He says He has done or will do something and then trusting Him to come through for you.

It's amazing how much we mothers trust our fellow humans and how little we trust God. When, fulfilling our role as family chauffeur, we pull out of our driveway, we have faith that other drivers will stay on the right side of the road and obey all the traffic laws. When we drop our children off at day care or school, we assume they will be safe and well cared for by the babysitters or teachers. When we head to our favorite family restaurant, we expect a good meal, not even considering that the cook could serve us salmonella-laced chicken.

Can you imagine going through life afraid to drive on the road because you believe all the other drivers are under the influence of alcohol? Or believing that anyone who works with kids does so with an ulterior motive in mind? Or going out to a restaurant and telling yourself, *I cannot eat this hamburger, for I am sure the cook has tainted it somehow.* Or going to your accountant and refusing to divulge any of your financial and personal information, saying, "If I tell you, I know you're going to steal my identity and run off to Cancun with my kid's college savings"? How about not going to Disney World to see the Magic Kingdom because, having seen neither, you don't believe they exist?

So how can we have faith in these strangers who are only human yet not have faith in God—the One who has power over all creation? And how can we have faith that other places on this planet exist without our ever having seen them, yet not have faith that *God* actually exists?

Because our thoughts lead us off course, we must continually look to God's Word, write it upon our hearts, and believe He will do as He has promised. We must imprint the words of Hebrews 11:1 upon our minds: "Faith makes us sure of what we hope for and gives us proof of what we cannot see" (CEV).

Perhaps you think you lack faith because you don't feel the working of the Holy Spirit in your life. In this regard, the fault lies in your lack of faith in God and His Word, not in the power of the Holy Spirit.

Fellow mothers, God is always ready to help—no matter who, what, when, where, or why. You must *believe*! Take it as fact that you never have to wait for Him to move—for He is patiently waiting for you to draw near and ask. In fact, *God Calling* tells us, "Your hour of need is the moment of my Coming."

Put your thoughts, then, over onto the side of faith. Say, "Lord, I will believe. I do believe," over and over again. Replace every suggestion of doubt—from within or without—with a statement of faith until, whether facing triumph or trial, you stand firm in your faith. Simply believe in His Word. Be certain He keeps His promises. And continually worship Him—through trial and triumph. Smith writes:

> *Dare to abandon yourself to the keeping and the saving power of the Lord Jesus. If you have ever trusted a precious interest in the hands of an earthly friend, I entreat you, trust yourself and all your spiritual interest now in the hands of your heavenly Friend, and never, never, never allow yourself to doubt again.*

Banish from your mind, worry, the one thing which is as totally incompatible to trust as oil is to water. Worry not only does not serve us, but also weakens us when we need all the strength we can garner for ourselves and our children.

Would that we could be as persevering in our faith, as strong in our belief as the Canaanite mother who encountered Jesus:

> *Jesus withdrew to the district of Tyre and Sidon.*
> *And behold, a woman who was a Canaanite from that district came out and, with a [loud, troublesomely urgent] cry, begged, Have mercy on me, O Lord, Son of David! My daughter is miserably and distressingly and cruelly possessed by a demon!*

But He did not answer her a word. And His disciples came and implored Him, saying, Send her away, for she is crying out after us.

He answered, I was sent only to the lost sheep of the house of Israel.

But she came and, kneeling, worshiped Him and kept praying, Lord, help me!

And He answered, It is not right (proper, becoming, or fair) to take the children's bread and throw it to the little dogs.

She said, Yes, Lord, yet even the little pups (little whelps) eat the crumbs that fall from their [young] masters' table.

Then Jesus answered her, O woman, great is your faith! Be it done for you as you wish. And her daughter was cured from that moment. (Matthew 15:21–28 AMP, emphasis added)

What an amazing account! This mother had heard about the miracles Jesus had been performing and so developed great faith in Him. And although she was a Gentile, she was determined to plead for her daughter's cause.

What mother who properly loved her child wouldn't beg for his or her deliverance? And notice that even when Jesus seemingly ignored her initial plea, she kept on coming to Him, kneeling down in humility and submission, continuing her prayer and her worship of Him! Because of this great faith, she learned the lesson of Matthew 7:7: "Keep on asking and it will be given you; keep on seeking and you will find; keep on knocking [reverently] and [the door] will be opened to you" (AMP).

May Jesus and others around us be as amazed with our faith as He was with this woman's! Isn't it amazing that the moment she exhibited her absolute and persistent faith, her daughter was healed? And not only healed instantly but from a distance, revealing that time and space cannot constrain the power of Jesus!

About this passage, *Matthew Henry's Commentary* states:

Though weak faith, if true, shall not be rejected, yet great faith shall be commended. . . . When our will conforms to the will of Christ's precept, his will concurs with the will of our desire. Those that will deny Christ nothing shall find that he will deny them nothing at last, though for a time he seems to hide his face from them. . . .

The mother's faith prevailed for the daughter's cure. He spake, and it was done.

The mother's faith won her daughter's remedy. She had patience and perseverance. But what Jesus commended was her great faith. Replace your doubting with knowing. Be as this woman—substituting fretting and fearing with firm faith. Smith writes:

It is a law of spiritual life that every act of trust makes the next act less difficult, until at length, if these acts are persisted in, trusting becomes, like breathing, the natural unconscious action of the redeemed soul.

Therefore put your will into your believing. Your faith must not be a passive imbecility but an active energy. You may have to believe against every appearance, but no matter.

Trust God in every little thing. Doing so will grow your hope, build your faith, and increase your peace so that when panic comes knocking on your door or the door of your child, you can answer it with unwavering trust in the Lord. Speak to it with God's words of faith, which you've written upon your heart. Reach for His calm. Don't allow the panicked thumping of your heart to drown out the words God is speaking into your life. Banish *dis*couragement—lack of courage—for it is a major impediment to your union with God.

Start with as much faith as the mustard seed (see Luke 17:6). "Do not despise these small beginnings, for the LORD rejoices to see the work begin" (Zechariah 4:10 NLT). Determinedly repeat to yourself, "I believe and trust in my Lord and His power." If you are patient and persistent in this, your worries will fade, your fears will wane, your faith will blossom, and you will share in the Lord's joy to the glory of God, who will say:

O woman [and O mother], great is thy faith.
MATTHEW 15:28 KJV

PATH MARKERS

Promise

I assure you, most solemnly I tell you, if anyone steadfastly believes in Me, he will himself be able to do the things that I do; and he will do even greater things than these, because I go to the Father.

JOHN 14:12 AMP

Proof

A leader of the local synagogue, whose name was Jairus, arrived. When he saw Jesus, he fell at his feet, pleading fervently with him. "My little daughter is dying," he said. "Please come and lay your hands on her; heal her so she can live."

Jesus went with him. . . .

Messengers arrived from the home of Jairus, the leader of the synagogue. They told him, "Your daughter is dead. There's no use troubling the Teacher now."

But Jesus overheard them and said to Jairus, "Don't be afraid. Just have faith." . . .

Holding her hand, he said to her, "Talitha koum," which means "Little girl, get up!" And the girl, who was twelve years old, immediately stood up and walked around! They were overwhelmed and totally amazed.

MARK 5:22–24, 35–36, 41–42 NLT

Provision

The apostles said to the Lord, "Increase our faith!" And the Lord said, "If you had faith like a mustard seed, you would say to this mulberry tree, 'Be uprooted and be planted in the sea'; and it would obey you."

LUKE 17:5–6 NASB

Portrait

In Christ, I live by faith, not by sight (see 2 Corinthians 5:7).

Mind-Renewing Prayers

Day 1

Joy Inexpressible

And though you have not seen Him, you love Him, and though
you do not see Him now, but believe in Him, you greatly
rejoice with joy inexpressible and full of glory.
1 Peter 1:8 NASB

Lord, some people say seeing is believing. But You ask us to believe without
seeing. That's what I'm working on. Because of Your Word, because of Your
promises, I know You are watching over my child. I know You are keeping us
both safe. Just like I comfort my child, You will always be there to comfort me.
Oh, what inexpressible joy!

Day 2

Forever on My Mind

Things that are seen don't last forever, but things that are not seen are eternal.
That's why we keep our minds on the things that cannot be seen.
2 Corinthians 4:18 cev

This world would have me believe all I can count on are the things around
me, things I can touch, see, and feel. But Jesus, when You came, You turned
the world upside down. The things unseen are what will last forever, what I can
depend on. And that's what I'm keeping my mind on—You, Your kingdom,
Your love for me and my child. What more could a mother want?

Day 3

Beyond My Comprehension

Now unto him that is able to do exceeding abundantly above
all that we ask or think, according to the power that worketh in us.
Ephesians 3:20 kjv

Lord, sometimes I think I limit the possibilities You have for me and my child
because my vision is inadequate. Keep reminding me that You are the Lord
of the impossible. That You are capable of finding a solution I'd never even
thought of. That You and Your ways are beyond my comprehension—and
that's a good thing! In You I find hope. In You my faith grows.

Day 4
Close to You

You will keep in perfect peace all who trust in you,
all whose thoughts are fixed on you!
ISAIAH 26:3 NLT

I believe, Lord! Help my unbelief! Whenever my thoughts drift away from Your presence, Your Word, Your Spirit, anxiety begins to take over. And that's not where I want to live. Help me stay close to You. I want Your perfect peace—for myself and my child. For when I am trusting in You, I find I am the mother You created me to be.

Day 5
Anything Is Possible

It was by faith that even Sarah was able to have a child,
though she was barren and was too old. She believed
that Go would keep his promise.
HEBREWS 11:11 NLT

Wow! I cannot imagine having a baby at the age of ninety! But that's what happens when a mother believes in You and Your promises, Lord. Anything is possible when we turn our eyes and give our hearts and dreams to You. That's a definite faith builder for me. I believe in You. I claim Your promises—as a woman of God, a mother of man, and a soul in Your keeping.

DAY 6

Blurred Vision

We don't yet see things clearly. We're squinting in a fog,
peering through a mist. But it won't be long before the weather
clears and the sun shines bright! We'll see it all then, see it all as
clearly as God sees us, knowing him directly just as he knows us!
1 CORINTHIANS 13:12 MSG

Sometimes, Lord, my vision blurs and I begin worrying about tomorrow. Will
I be able to provide for my children through thick and thin? Will they turn out
to be the people I hoped they would be? Will they keep their faith in You? Help
me leave all these questions in Your hands. Help me be okay with not having
all the answers. Help me simply have faith in You.

DAY 7

Reveling in the Joy!

Now the God of hope fill you with all joy and peace in believing,
that ye may abound in hope, through the power of the Holy Ghost.
ROMANS 15:13 KJV

What joy! What peace I have—when I put all my faith in You. Gone are the
nagging what-ifs. Banished are the sleepless nights. You are the God of hope.
And I revel in the joy of being Your daughter. I place all I am and have—
including myself and my children—in Your hands. And leave us there!

Chapter 7

Challenges concerning the Will

Then said [Christiana's friend] Mercy—
Let the Most Blessed be my guide,
If't be His blessed will;
Unto His gate, into His fold,
Up to His holy hill.
And let Him never suffer me
To swerve or turn aside
From His free grace, and holy ways,
Whate'er shall me betide.
JOHN BUNYAN, *THE PILGRIM'S PROGRESS: PART 2*

• • • • • • •

*S*o now here we are, mothers who have stepped out in faith. We are finding joy as we trust God and live hidden in Christ. We are just beginning to perceive the blessings of such a union when another challenge meets us on our soul's pathway. For although we have experienced Christ's peace and rest, both may begin to wane as we wonder if we are truly walking in God's will or are merely nothing more than hypocrites or pretenders.

At this point, we have once again begun to rely upon our emotions instead of the truth of God. If we consider that the life hidden in Christ is lived in the things we feel, all our attention is focused on our emotions rather than where it belongs—on Jesus.

We know our emotions are as volatile as the stock market—especially with the hormone swings we undergo from the what's-happening-to-my-body confusion of puberty to the if-I-blossom-any-more-I-may-explode feelings of pregnancy to the no-one-is-going-to-kick-me-around-anymore attitude of postmenopause. When we are riding high, when things are going well, when our direction and purpose are certain and we feel our kids are finally on the right track, our life of faith seems real. But when we are at our lowest point, confused as to what our next step should be, frightened for our kids' future, wondering if things could get any worse, we feel we may not have surrendered ourselves to God's will at all. At this juncture, we must fall back upon the truth that the life in Christ is not lived in the emotions but in the will. And if we keep our wills consistently abiding in their center—which is God's will, the true reality—our emotional ups and downs will not disturb us. But how do we get there from here?

First, we must realize that when we are not walking in God's will, there is dissonance, for only when our will is tied to His, and His will obeyed, will harmony reign within us. That is when the Holy Spirit truly begins to gently guide us into right living.

Although our emotions belong to us and are tolerated and enjoyed by us, they are not our true selves. They are not who we actually are. Thus, if our God is to take hold of us, it must be into this central will or personality that He enters in. Then if He is reigning within that central will by the power of His Spirit, all the rest of that personality must come under His influence. For as the will goes, so does the woman.

Second, we must again shift our will to the believing side, for when we choose to *believe*, we need not worry about how we *feel*. If you believe God has the best plan for you and your children, your emotions will eventually be compelled to come into the harmony of the real you, the woman hidden in Christ, the authentic you, in the secret place of the Father!

To get some idea of how a mother's will can get in God's way, let's check out Rebekah. At the beginning of her story in Genesis, she showed her great faith in God by going off with Abraham's servant to meet and marry a man she'd never met. Because that man, Isaac, was also her second cousin, he was truly a "relative" stranger.

After twenty years of marriage, Rebekah finally conceived and found herself with twins, a double blessing from God. Her great faith and trust in God, His will, and His way was confirmed when she, the first woman the Bible records as making a direct plea to God, asked Him why her twins were struggling within her. His response was that her twins represented two nations that would be at odds with each other, and He also promised that the older would eventually be servant to the younger.

The boys, first Esau and then Jacob, were born. Esau became his father Isaac's favorite and Jacob the apple of Rebekah's eye. Here is where Rebekah, a once-faithful follower of God, began to doubt God's promises and so went against God's will by taking matters into her own hands. A proud mother determined to get her own way for her favorite, regardless of what God may have had in mind, let the emotions of fear and doubt overtake her. She coerced Jacob to join her in deceiving her husband so that Isaac would be tricked into giving Esau's blessing to Jacob. Edith Deen, author of *All the Women of the Bible*, writes:

> *We cannot make any excuses for Rebekah's actions in deceiving her blind husband and at the same time influencing her son in what was wrong. But may we not say that, though her actions were morally indefensible, her motive was pure? Does she not typify the mother down the ages who, weak in faith, imagines herself to be carrying out the will of God?*

Notice the words *weak in faith*. That's what often leads us into going with what we think best—and not with what God thinks best. For Rebekah, the result of her actions was manifold.

- She took on the blame or "curse" for this deception. (See Genesis 27:13.)
- Esau threatened to murder his brother Jacob. (See Genesis 27:41.)
- Isaac sent Jacob away from home, and Rebekah never laid eyes on him again. (See Genesis 27:43.)
- The last years of her life were spent with a husband who probably felt he could no longer trust his wife and with a son, Esau, who felt betrayed.

So how does a once-faithful woman of God get so far out of God's will—not only for her life but for the lives of her children? By allowing her motherly emotions and designs for her children's success to override God's wisdom and ways. In *Effective Parenting in a Defective World*, Chip Ingram writes:

> *Remember that you are not called to produce successful, upwardly mobile, highly educated, athletically talented machines. . . . Giving your children great opportunities is good; it is not, however, the goal of parenting. Christlikeness is. Above all, seek to raise children who look and act a lot like Jesus.*

And to be like Christ, we and our children must say to God, "I want your will to be done, not mine" (Luke 22:42 NLT). Although at times we may find great difficulty in controlling our emotions, we *can* control our wills. So we may say firmly and continually, "I give my will to God," for deep inside, we know He *always* knows best.

Hannah Whitall Smith provides a wonderful analogy in regard to the will, likening it to a wise mother in a nursery:

> *The feelings are like a set of clamoring, crying children. The mother, knowing that she is the authority figure, pursues her course lovingly and calmly in spite of all their clamors. The result is that the children are sooner or later won over to the mother's course of action and fall in with her decisions, and all is harmonious and happy. But if that mother should for a moment let in the thought that the children were the masters instead of herself, confusion would reign unchecked. In how many souls at this very moment is there nothing but confusion, simply because the feelings are allowed to govern instead of the will?*
>
> *The real thing in your experience is what your will decides, not your emotions. You are far more in danger of hypocrisy and untruth in yielding to the assertions of your feelings than in holding fast to the decision of your will.*

Are your emotions leading you astray and, in turn, your children? Are your thoughts convincing you that you are a hypocrite, making you feel ashamed? If so, stop. Take a deep breath and rein in your feelings. Then take those thoughts of hypocrisy away, captive to the obedience of Christ (see 2 Corinthians 10:5). Our powerful emotions are proud obstacles that can be pulled down by the truth of the Gospel through the power, grace, mercy, and love of God.

When we say to the Lord, "You are my hiding place. You protect me from trouble. You surround me with joyous songs of salvation" (Psalm 32:7 GW), He says:

> *"I will instruct you. I will teach you the way that you should go. I will advise you as my eyes watch over you. Don't be stubborn like a horse or mule. They need a bit and bridle in their mouth to restrain them, or they will not come near you."* (Psalm 32:8–9 GW)

And what happens if we do *not* cling stubbornly to our own will? Instead of suffering the repercussions of insisting our will be done, we will be surrounded by mercy. We will "be glad and find joy in the Lord" (Psalm 32:11 GW). We will find ourselves bursting out in song, so great will our happiness be!

Thus, our joy will be found when we remain in God's will. But how do we find God's will for our lives? By continually coming to Him in prayer, by consistently immersing ourselves in His Word, by constantly seeking Him first (see Luke 11:9–10).

Seeking His will in all facets of life is a constant, consistent practice on our part. We are to continue asking, seeking, and knocking. In doing so, we will continue to receive God in our hearts and find His will for our lives. And He will keep on opening doors that had been shut!

But you may ask, "If I follow God's will, how will my family, friends, and loved ones fare?" Not to worry, for He has promised that if we seek God's kingdom first, everything else will fall in line; all will be provided (see Luke 12:29–32).

When we live in God's will and are hidden in Christ, we take up residence in the worry-free zone, a place where emotions amount to naught, where they become mere specks of dust floating on the surfaces of our minds.

We cannot wrestle with God's will. If we do, we will end up limping around like Jacob. But when our wills work with God's, we are indeed powers to be reckoned with! And this is amazing because it is what we were created to do from the very beginning. Before the fall of man, our natural state was in total harmony with God. We're just getting right back to the beginning!

We must keep in mind that in following God's will for our lives, we may not always see the picture or the outcome He has in mind for ourselves or our children. In *The Mentor Quest*, Betty Southard writes:

> *We all get caught up in the daily details of life, and it can hinder our seeing the bigger plan God has for us. Our immediate problems overwhelm us and seem to obliterate God's promises. God, on the other hand, sees the bigger picture and wants us to focus in on what he is accomplishing in our lives. God's lessons are surrounding us daily, if only we are willing to set aside our business and open our "eyes to see and ears to hear."*

In the midst of our daily activities, we do not need to know or understand all that God is doing. We need merely to take a step back, open our "eyes to see and ears to hear," focus on Jesus, and look for signs of the Holy Spirit's movement. We need not fear God's will but *trust* Him, resting in the truth that He knows what He's doing.

So consider your emotions as merely servants and regard your will in God's as the real master of your being. When you do, you'll find you can ignore your emotions—even when they are in regard to your children—and simply pay attention to the state of your will. Each day, present yourself to God as a living sacrifice. Trust Him to move in your life. Dispose of the Mom-is-always-right attitude. Keep in mind, as Smith tells us, that we are not giving up our wills but are simply substituting the "higher, divine, mature will of God for our foolish, misdirected wills of ignorance and immaturity":

He wills that you should be entirely surrendered to Him and that you should trust Him perfectly. If you have taken the steps of surrender and faith in your will, it is your right to believe that no matter how much your feelings may clamor against it, you are all the Lord's, and He has begun to "worketh in you both to will and to do of his good pleasure" [Philippians 2:13 KJV].

$\mathcal{P}$ATH MARKERS

$\mathcal{P}$romise

This. . .says the Lord: I will imprint My laws upon their hearts, and I will inscribe them on their minds (on their inmost thoughts and understanding).

HEBREWS 10:16 AMP

$\mathcal{P}$roof

Paul and his friends went through Phrygia and Galatia, but the Holy Spirit would not let them preach in Asia. After they arrived in Mysia, they tried to go into Bithynia, but the Spirit of Jesus would not let them. So they went on through Mysia until they came to Troas.

During the night, Paul had a vision of someone from Macedonia who was standing there and begging him, "Come over to Macedonia and help us!" After Paul had seen the vision, we began looking for a way to go to Macedonia. We were sure that God had called us to preach the good news there.

ACTS 16:6–10 CEV

$\mathcal{P}$rovision

I am telling you nothing but the truth when I say it is profitable (good, expedient, advantageous) for you that I go away. Because if I do not go away, the Comforter (Counselor, Helper, Advocate, Intercessor, Strengthener, Standby) will not come to you [into close fellowship with you]; but if I go away, I will send Him to you [to be in close fellowship with you].

JOHN 16:7 AMP

In Christ, I have access to God's will (see 1 John 5:14).

MIND-RENEWING PRAYERS

DAY 1
In Your Will

In Christ we were chosen to be God's people, because from the very beginning God had decided this in keeping with his plan. And he is the One who makes everything agree with what he decides and wants.

EPHESIANS 1:11 NCV

Honestly, Lord, sometimes it's just so hard to remember that You have a plan, that You know better, especially when it comes to my children. Help me to continually keep my eyes on You, to stop and ask Your will before I make any decision. And remind me that, when I feel dissonance, it's time to confer once again with You to make sure I'm in Your will and not in Your way.

Day 2
Children of God

We pray that you will lead a life that is worthy of the Lord.
We pray that you will please him in every way. So we want you
to bear fruit in every good thing you do. We want you to grow to
know God better. We want you to be very strong, in keeping with his
glorious power. We want you to be patient. Never give up. Be joyful.
COLOSSIANS 1:10–11 NIrV

I am so excited about trusting You with decisions, Lord. This seems to be
a burden I've carried far too long. May I, by walking in Your way, be an
example to my children. Give me the wisdom and the courage to teach them
how to find their own way in Your will. And may each of us be blessed and
pleasing to You as we, children of God, all grow up in You.

Day 3
Seeds of Untruth

[We] refute arguments and theories and reasonings and every
proud and lofty thing that sets itself up against the [true] knowledge
of God; and we lead every thought and purpose away captive into
the obedience of Christ (the Messiah, the Anointed One).
2 CORINTHIANS 10:5 AMP

The world plants so many seeds of untruth in my mind, Lord. And sometimes
I don't know how to respond. But what I do know is that You want my thoughts
on higher things. You want me to take refuge in You and Your Word. So, Lord,
in this very moment, help me to discern what You would have me think and
do. Bless me with the knowledge and wisdom of God the Father.

Day 4
Complete Harmony

*There's a day coming when the mountain of God's House will
be The Mountain—solid, towering over all mountains.
All nations will river toward it, people from all over set out for it.
They'll say, "Come, let's climb God's Mountain, go to the House of the God of
Jacob. He'll show us the way he works so we can live the way we're made."*
ISAIAH 2:2–3 MSG

Lord, I want to live how You originally made us. I'm so tired of messing up because I went with my *own* plans based on how I was feeling at the time. I want to be in complete harmony with You. I want to revel in the freedom that comes with matching my will with Yours. Show me the way, Lord. Spread Your light across my path.

Day 5
A God-Scan

*God, see what is in my heart. Know what is there. Put me to the test.
Know what I'm thinking. See if there's anything in my life you don't like.
Help me live in the way that is always right.*
PSALM 139:23–24 NIrV

*I—mind, body, spirit, and soul—come to You, Lord. Give me a God-scan.
Show me where I have fallen short. Lift me with Your righteous hand. Keep a
firm grip on me. Give me the strength to trust You with my children, the lights
of my life, to bring them to You and leave them in Your hands.*

DAY 6
Humble, Then Honest

*If any of you lack wisdom, let him ask of God, that giveth to all
men liberally, and upbraideth not; and it shall be given him.*
JAMES 1:5 KJV

*I'm so tired of trying to live this life under my own power. Of worrying. Of
doing what I think is best for me and my children without even consulting
You. This plan is not working out—at all. So I come to You today, God, for
wisdom, instruction, direction. Help me be humble, then honest with my
children, to let them know I don't have all the answers—but You do!*

DAY 7
In Your Eyes

*Remember the LORD in all you do,
and he will give you success.*
PROVERBS 3:6 NCV

*In each and every moment of the day, Lord, may I be living, working, and
loving for You. May You continually be at the forefront of my mind, not back
in the dark recesses. I want to put You first in my life, for then all else will fall
into place. Make me a success in Your eyes—and help my children to do the
same, for Your glory!*

CHAPTER 8
Challenges concerning Guidance

The Pilgrims desired, with trembling, to go forward; only they prayed their guide to strike a light, that they might go the rest of their way by the help of the light, of a lantern. So he struck a light, and they went by the help of that through the rest of this way, though the darkness was very great [2 Peter 1:19].
JOHN BUNYAN, *THE PILGRIM'S PROGRESS: PART 2*

• • • • • • •

*H*ere you are, on the beginning steps of the pathway to a life of faith and joy. You have totally given yourself to God—mind, body, soul, and spirit. You are determined to keep yourself in His hands, and He is shaping you into a new creature with a divine purpose. You have determined to keep your will in agreement with His, to obey Him in all things, and to trust Him with everything. You are certain that, although He may lead you down challenging paths, God, in His wisdom, knows what's best for you. But now you may be unsure of the next step. You know God has a purpose for your life, but in which direction should you go?

At this juncture, you must be certain of two things, the first of which is that the Father, Son, and Holy Spirit are determined to make their will known to you and to guide you down the right path—every step of the way. In fact, they have promised to do so! When you ask God for wisdom, He will give it freely (see James 1:5). Jesus will make sure you know His voice (see John 10:3–4). And the Holy Spirit will teach you everything you need to know and show you every path you need to go (see John 14:26)!

With the Father, Son, and Holy Spirit on your side, you cannot get lost or fear anything. If you confidently believe in them, if you determine to look for and expect their guidance, you will receive it. But you must not doubt:

> *Only it must be in faith that he asks with no wavering (no hesitating, no doubting). For the one who wavers (hesitates, doubts) is like the billowing surge out at sea that is blown hither and thither and tossed by the wind. (James 1:6 AMP)*

The second thing of which you must be certain is that God knows absolutely everything! So regardless of how you or those around you see confusion and loss in the path He has chosen for you, He knows exactly what blessings await you. Although you may not understand His road map for you, remember that with your human vision, you see only a portion of the map. He sees the entire picture, and in His vision you must trust, as easily as you trust your GPS.

Jesus has told us, "Anyone who comes to me but refuses to let go of father, mother, spouse, children, brothers, sisters—yes, even one's own self!—can't be my disciple" (Luke 14:26–27 MSG). This is a hard statement for most moms to swallow, especially the part about letting go of children. But it is God's truth that upon our pathways, we may discover that to follow Jesus, we are called to forsake inwardly *everyone* in our lives—including ourselves and our children! In other words, we may be guided to paths that those we love most will disapprove of. For this we must be prepared. We must continually tell ourselves God is in control. He knows all—including what's best, regardless of appearances or opinions.

But how does God give us His guidance? In four simple "ways": through (1) His Word, (2) providential circumstances, (3) our own higher judgment, and (4) the inward promptings of the Holy Spirit. When these four are all in sync, we know God's hand is guiding us.

Way 1: *Through His Word.* If your road map bypasses scripture, look out, Mama—you are headed for a dead end. If you are confused about which path to take, consult God's Word (see 2 Timothy 3:16–17). If the Bible provides guidance in that particular regard, ask the Holy Spirit to make everything clear to you. Then obey. But be careful not to take scripture out of context just because that's the answer or the guidance you endeavor to have.

And remember that although the Bible tells us what kind of person we should marry (see 1 Corinthians 7:39), it doesn't give us a name. Although it tells us how we should work (see Colossians 3:17, 23–24), it doesn't tell us what specific occupation we should have. And although it gives us pointers on how to raise our children (see Proverbs 22:6; Ephesians 6:4), it doesn't reveal whether we should ground a teenager—or for how long! In those cases and others, if you cannot find a clear answer in the Bible, seek guidance using the other three ways mentioned— through circumstances, your intelligence, and the Spirit's prompting. If any of these tests fails, you need to stop. Wait on the Lord. Watch for Him to move. Eventually He will give you the wisdom you seek.

Way 2: *Through providential circumstances.* Next we can look at what's happening in our lives, the providential circumstances that have come to the forefront. For instance, you may have been somewhat content being a stay-at-home mom, only to find your husband gets laid off. You thought your duty was clear but now find yourself not knowing which way to turn. Yet now you can perhaps do the thing you had wanted to do for a long time, such as leave your hubby in charge of the kids while *you* go back to work outside of the home. God has, in effect, pushed you out of your comfort zone so that you will be moved to do what He has clearly called you to do, perhaps years ago!

If our circumstances are truly providential, God will open doors for us—we won't have to break them down. In other words, if our direction is truly from God, He will go before us and pave the way.

Way 3: *Through our own higher judgment.* The third way is to utilize our God-given gifts and intelligence, which God wants us to use to find our pathway (see Psalm 32:8–9; Matthew 22:37). Although we are not to depend on our own unenlightened reasoning or common sense, we can use *spiritually* enlightened judgment to find our way, for God will speak to us through the abilities He has given us. In other words, if we are tone deaf, He will not call upon us to be on the worship team.

Way 4: *Through the inward promptings of the Holy Spirit.* The final way to find God's guidance is following cues given by the Holy Spirit. If you sense the Spirit putting up roadblocks, prompting you to stop dead in your tracks—stop! Wait until all barriers are removed before forging ahead.

But if your barrier is merely fear, if you are uncomfortable about a new endeavor or direction, that may not be the Holy Spirit saying to stop. It may simply mean that God is about to stretch you spiritually and mentally or is about to pull you back from a path on which you may have strayed.

At the same time, you must be aware that dissonance of the divine harmony within you might not be coming from God but from other sources. The strong personalities in our lives influence us greatly. So do our temporal circumstances and conditions, which sway us more than we know. In these instances, our worldly desire for a particular thing may override (or threaten to override) God's guiding voice.

Now that we have the litmus test of God's guidance in place, let's look at Lot's wife whose disregard of God's promptings led to her demise. Genesis tells us she had followed her affluent husband, Lot, into the city of Sodom where they lived with her two married daughters. She most likely had a beautiful home and lots of wonderful clothes to wear because when the two angels of God came to rescue her and her family from the destruction of Sodom, they had to *drag* her out of the city:

> *The angels became insistent. "Hurry," they said to Lot. "Take your wife and your two daughters who are here. Get out right now, or you will be swept away in the destruction of the city!"*
>
> *When Lot still hesitated, the angels seized his hand and the hands of his wife and two daughters and rushed them to safety outside the city, for the LORD was merciful. When they were safely out of the city, one of the angels ordered, "Run for your lives! And don't look back or stop anywhere in the valley!" (Genesis 19:15–17 NLT)*

Just when the family reached safety, the Lord did indeed destroy Sodom. But here is where Lot's wife's true character is revealed as a mother whose love of her affluent home and hearth in Sodom was more powerful than her obedience to or love for God, for "Lot's wife looked back as she was following behind him, and she turned into a pillar of salt" (Genesis 19:26 NLT).

Lot's wife is a heart-stopping example of a mother who ignored:

- God's word and warnings—spoken from the mouths of His angels, no less

- her circumstances—a God-paved pathway she ultimately refused to continue on
- her own intelligence—the passion for her home fogged up her brain cells
- God's spiritual guides—the fervent pleas of two heavenly angels.

The results? She not only turned into a pillar of salt, but her now-widowed daughters, left to their own devices, ensured the continuance of their father's line by having relations with him and becoming pregnant. These daughters were a reflection of their mother's own beliefs, desires, and values. What a plethora of examples *not* to follow!

Although a spiritual enemy did not seem in force here, the devil is another source whose influence may cause us disharmony. We all know what happened with Eve in the garden when she listened to the wrong voice, leading to her—and the world's—fall.

Thus, it's not enough to *feel* you are being led to a new endeavor or action. You must *discern* the source of the voice calling you before you rush off down the path. Step back. Take the time to find the true voice—no matter how long you may have to wait. Listen carefully. Then when you hear the Spirit say, "This is the right path. Walk in it," move out (see Isaiah 30:21). When you do, know for a certainty that Jesus, the Good Shepherd, is leading the way, for you are obeying His command to follow Him.

Endeavor to discern God's guidance by using, along with these four tests, what Smith calls "a divine sense of 'oughtness' derived from the harmony of all God's voices." When you do, you will have nothing to fear. If you have faith in Him, if you trust Him with all, you will have the courage and strength to walk the way He is leading, your hand in His.

There is no fear for those living this higher life if they live each moment of every day under God's guidance. It is the most wonderful privilege and promise we have been given and leads to a myriad of rewards.

"Rejoice in it. Embrace it eagerly," Smith writes. "Let everything go that it may be yours."

And remember that your children are watching every move you make. Your example of going to God for guidance will teach them how to do the same. That's a wonderful legacy for any mother to leave in her children's hands.

"Remember what happened to Lot's wife!
If you cling to your life, you will lose it,
and if you let your life go, you will save it!"
LUKE 17:32–33 NLT

$\mathscr{P}$ATH MARKERS

....

$\mathscr{P}$romise

I will instruct you and teach you in the way you should go; I will guide you with My eye.

PSALM 32:8 NKJV

$\mathscr{P}$roof

In this way, they traveled and camped at the LORD's command wherever he told them to go. . . . Whether the cloud stayed above the Tabernacle for two days, a month, or a year, the people of Israel stayed in camp and did not move on. But as soon as it lifted, they broke camp and moved on. So they camped or traveled at the LORD's command, and they did whatever the LORD told them through Moses.

NUMBERS 9:18, 22–23 NLT

$\mathscr{P}$rovision

Every Scripture passage is inspired by God. All of them are useful for teaching, pointing out errors, correcting people, and training them for a life that has God's approval.

2 TIMOTHY 3:16 GW

$\mathscr{P}$ortrait

In Christ, I have access to God's wisdom and direction (see 1 Corinthians 1:30).

Mind-Renewing Prayers

Day 1
Speak, Lord

Your ears shall hear a word behind you, saying, "This is the way, walk in it,"
whenever you turn to the right hand or whenever you turn to the left.
ISAIAH 30:21 NKJV

Lord, I have a decision to make but I'm not sure which way to go, which road to take. Give me Your wisdom. Help me to draw away from the clamor of my household so that I can hear Your voice clearly. Show me the way. Speak, Lord, I'm listening.

Day 2
Solid Ground

If you do what the LORD wants, he will make certain each step you take is sure.
The LORD will hold your hand, and if you stumble, you still won't fall.
PSALM 37:23–24 CEV

Make Your will and guidance for me clear, God. Make the desires of my heart align with Yours. When I'm in sync with You, I know each step I take will be on solid ground. Lead me by the hand, Lord. Take me to the rock that is higher than I, where the air is clear, the view perfect, and my safety assured.

Day 3
Waiting for the Way

Wait and hope for and expect the Lord; be brave and of good courage and let your heart be stout and enduring. Yes, wait for and hope for and expect the Lord.
PSALM 27:14 AMP

I'm waiting on You, Lord. I'm expecting You to show me the way to go, the path to take. I'm looking for You in Your Word and my circumstances. I'm staying attuned to the Holy Spirit and using my enlightened judgment to discern Your will. And as I wait, I know You will give me the courage to stay where I am until I know Your way for certain.

Day 4
Running to You

Trust GOD from the bottom of your heart; don't try to figure out everything on your own. Listen for GOD's voice in everything you do, everywhere you go; he's the one who will keep you on track. Don't assume that you know it all. Run to GOD!
PROVERBS 3:5–7 MSG

Here I am, Lord, running to You, seeking Your light for my path. I am waiting for Your wisdom, the Spirit's help, and Jesus' nudge. Help me to be patient. Open Your Word to my heart, spirit, and soul. Show me Your plan. Open my ears to Your voice in all that I say and do.

DAY 5

In Your Hands

"For I know the plans I have for you," says the LORD.
"They are plans for good and not for disaster,
to give you a future and a hope."
JEREMIAH 29:11 NLT

I love to make plans, Lord—not just for myself but for everyone in my life. And when those plans are ruined, I get frustrated. But I know *You* are concerned with every detail of my life. And I know You have a grand scheme for each and every one of us. Your plan is supreme, so no matter what happens, I can relax in hope, knowing everything and everyone is in Your hands.

DAY 6

Dreams in My Heart

May He grant you according to your heart's
desire and fulfill all your plans.
PSALM 20:4 AMP

You know the desires of my heart, Lord. In fact, no one, not even myself, knows me better than You do. So here I am, in Your presence, hoping my will is the same as Your will for my life. For then I will know the dreams in my heart are true, were planted there by You, and are about to come into fruition. How cool is that?

Day 7
Walking Your Pathway

*Thus says the Lord: Stand by the roads and look;
and ask for the eternal paths, where the good, old way is;
then walk in it, and you will find rest for your souls.*
JEREMIAH 6:16 AMP

I'm at a crossroads, Lord, waiting for direction from You. Pour Your wisdom upon me. Keep my heart, mind, and soul attentive to Your way. Once I have Your guidance, Your blessing, I pray I will have the strength and courage to do what You have called me to do. For when I'm walking Your pathway, I will have Your cherished peace and love.

CHAPTER 9
Challenges concerning Doubts

*Mr. Great-heart said, I have a commandment to resist sin,
to overcome evil, to fight the good fight of faith;
and, I pray, with whom should I fight this good fight,
if not with Giant Despair? I will, therefore, attempt the taking
away of his life, and the demolishing of Doubting Castle.*
JOHN BUNYAN, *THE PILGRIM'S PROGRESS: PART 2*

• • • • • • •

Although Christians are sometimes called believers—because we have faith in God, having no doubt in His existence—many of us could be called doubters. This may be because we do not have an active, personal relationship with Christ. Instead, we have merely a surface faith. We believe in God up to a point, a point where we can stay safe and comfortable. But once we are stretched beyond that point—which, for many of us, happens on the day we become moms—we may begin to doubt a bit, for our lives have instantly become untenable. Having kids can be like standing on a ledge, struggling to keep not only our own balance but theirs as well.

It may even be that, at some point, we become uncertain that God even likes us, much less loves us. We may hesitate to say that we have been forgiven totally, that our destiny is indeed heaven. In such cases, we neither feel nor display the hope of the life hidden in Christ, and it seems as if we have resigned ourselves to lives of misery, bereft of joy, accepting this as our lot.

Some other moms, assured that their sins are forgiven and they are destined for heaven, may be a little farther on the journey. They seem certain of their future but still have doubts about their present. They either do not believe in or are not versed in the myriad promises God has spoken of and provided for those who believe. Or being modern moms, they doubt the promises God made thousands of years ago can possibly apply to their lives today! For them, seeing is believing—and what they currently see of the world fills them, and in turn their children, with misgivings. As a result, they have no hope or joy in their present day and so live in the future instead of the moment.

The instant we let doubts enter our minds, our fight of faith ends. Whatever joy we had flies out the window, and our spiritual rebellion begins. For when we doubt, we are calling God, Jesus, and the Holy Spirit liars, for "he that believeth not God hath made him a liar" (1 John 5:10 kjv)!

In Hannah Whitall Smith's comparison of faith and doubt, she writes:

> *I remember seeing once the indignation and sorrow of a mother's heart deeply stirred by a little doubting on the part of one of her children. She had brought two little girls to my house, to leave them while she did some errands. One of them, with the happy confidence of childhood, abandoned herself to all the pleasures she could find in my nursery and sang and played until her mother's return. The other one, with the wretched caution and mistrust of maturity, sat down alone in a corner to wonder, first, whether her mother would remember to come back for her and to fear she would be forgotten and then to imagine her mother would be glad of the chance to get rid of her anyhow because she was such a naughty girl; and ended with working herself up into a perfect frenzy of despair. The look on that mother's face, when upon her return the weeping little girl told what was the matter with her, I shall not easily forget. Grief, wounded love, indignation, and pity all strove together for mastery: and the mother hardly knew who was most at fault, herself or the child, that such doubts should be possible.*

Perhaps you feel like the second child in the nursery, unworthy of receiving the promises of God. Perhaps you have sinned to the point of believing God would be well rid of you. Perhaps you have undergone so many trials you are convinced that, for some reason, God has forsaken you and no longer cares about you or your life.

Moms, if you have entertained such thoughts and doubts, be assured: Father God came to save us. In fact, He has told us that He "came to call not the righteous, but sinners to repentance." Smith writes, "Your very sinfulness and unworthiness, instead of being a reason why He should not love you and care for you, are really your chief claim upon His love and His care"! What a wonderful truth to meditate on. He truly does care for and love us, and shame on us for doubting such lavish care and love.

Any accusations that come into our heads about our behavior and mistakes come from one source—the enemy. He brings charges against us day and night (see Revelation 12:10). And if we listen to—and believe—his case against us, we find ourselves in agreement with him. The only things then left are doubt and discouragement, which lead to the darkness of Giant Despair, who not only imprisons us but keeps us from growing in our faith. The keys to unlock the doors of Doubting Castle? Those Jesus Christ gave us! We have "complete and free access to God's kingdom, keys to open any and every door: no more barriers between heaven and earth, earth and heaven" (Matthew 16:19 MSG).

Yet perhaps we're sometimes embarrassed, even ashamed, to admit to Jesus that we have doubts. So instead of praying about them, we suppress them. On this despairing heap, we add guilt as a sort of cherry on top, making ourselves even more miserable and distancing ourselves farther from God. Or perhaps we are afraid, like Sarah who laughed when God told her she would be a mother (see Genesis 18:12–15).

Fellow moms, if you are doubting God's ability to do the impossible—stop! Put your eyes back on Jesus. Look to the promises in God's Word. They are for *all* of us, and they never fail. "Not a single one of all the good promises the LORD had given to the family of Israel was left unfulfilled; everything he had spoken came true" (Joshua 21:45 NLT).

Consider the Old Testament character referred to as the Shunammite woman. She was accustomed to inviting a man of God, the prophet Elisha, to dinner whenever he passed through her town. After consulting with her husband, they had a little room built onto their home for Elisha so that he had a place to stay whenever he came by. To repay this childless woman for her generosity, Elisha asked her what he could do for her. Although she was apparently a woman of faith, she may not have wanted to be stretched in that faith, for in her response she told him, "Nothing. I'm secure and satisfied in my family" (2 Kings 4:13 MSG). Then his servant helped him come up with an idea:

> *Elisha said to her, "This time next year you're going to be nursing an infant son."*
>
> *"O my master, O Holy Man," she said, "don't play games with me, teasing me with such fantasies!" The woman conceived. A year later, just as Elisha had said, she had a son. (2 Kings 4:16–17 MSG)*

What a miracle! A newborn son. Years went by and all was well, until one day the boy, stricken with a headache, died in her arms. Yet not once did the Shunammite, an intensely driven mother, doubt the man of God would make things right. First she calmly set her son's lifeless body down in Elisha's room. Then she told her husband, "It will be all right." She then instructed her driver, "Ride fast; do not slacken your pace for me unless I tell you. So she set out and came to the man of God" (2 Kings 4:24–25 AMP). Seeing the Shunammite woman in the distance, Elisha's servant Gehazi ran out to meet her. When he asked her what was wrong, she once more responded with, "It is well" (v. 26), and continued moving forward to Elisha. When she finally reached him, she clung to his feet. She never told him her son was dead but asked, "Did I desire a son of my lord? Did I not say, Do not deceive me?" (2 Kings 4:28 AMP). In response, Elisha quickly sent his servant ahead. But the Shunammite woman stayed behind, saying to Elisha, "As the Lord lives and as my soul lives, I will not leave you" (2 Kings 4:30 AMP).

As the story goes, this woman's faith was rewarded by Elisha bringing her son back to life, at which point she "came and fell at his feet, bowing herself to the ground. Then she took up her son and went out" (2 Kings 4:37 AMP).

May it be that *we* would have such faith. That we, as mothers who love our children—and even more, love and trust our God and His promises—would build a room within ourselves for Jesus, our Man of God and Son of God. A place where He would abide, sup with us, and share our lives. He has already stretched our faith by making us mothers. Now would we allow Him to grow our faith by continuing to trust in Him—no matter what happens in our lives! Oswald Chambers writes, "Faith is deliberate confidence in the character of God whose ways you may not understand at the time." Do you have that confidence in God?

Fellow moms, having had children, we're *already* living on the edge. Why not recognize that God is living there right along with us? Why not acknowledge and affirm He is within our hearts—no matter what happens? Keep the faith that God, in His love, will always work to enlarge or stretch your faith.

If you have doubts, surrender them to Jesus. Tell Him, "I do believe; help me overcome my unbelief!" (Mark 9:24 TNIV). He will remind you not only that nothing is impossible for Him; that "no word from God will ever fail" (Luke 1:37 TNIV); that His word always produces fruit, accomplishes what He wants, prospers everywhere He sends it (see Isaiah 55:11); but also that "everything is possible for one who *believes*!" (Mark 9:23 TNIV, emphasis added).

When doubts begin creeping back in, do not despair. Turn them over to the Lord. Protect yourself with the shield of faith. Arm yourself with "the sword of the Spirit, which is the word of God" (Ephesians 6:17 TNIV). By reciting God's promises (mentally or aloud)—which you, daughter of God, have inherited—you will be putting your focus back where it belongs: on Jesus.

So God has given both his promise and his oath. These two things are
unchangeable because it is impossible for God to lie. Therefore,
we who have fled to him for refuge can have great confidence as we hold
to the hope that lies before us. This hope is a strong
and trustworthy anchor for our souls.
HEBREWS 6:18–19 NLT

PATH MARKERS

Promise

"God is not like people. He tells no lies. He is not like humans. He doesn't change his mind. When he says something, he does it. When he makes a promise, he keeps it."

NUMBERS 23:19 GW

Proof

"You unbelieving generation," Jesus replied, "how long shall I stay with you? How long shall I put up with you? Bring the boy to me."

So they brought him. When the spirit saw Jesus, it immediately threw the boy into a convulsion. He fell to the ground and rolled around, foaming at the mouth.

Jesus asked the boy's father, "How long has he been like this?"

"From childhood," he answered. "It has often thrown him into fire or water to kill him. But if you can do anything, take pity on us and help us."

" 'If you can'?" said Jesus. "Everything is possible for one who believes."

Immediately the boy's father exclaimed, "I do believe; help me overcome my unbelief!"

When Jesus saw that a crowd was running to the scene, he rebuked the impure spirit. "You deaf and mute spirit," he said, "I command you, come out of him and never enter him again."

The spirit shrieked, convulsed him violently and came out. The boy looked so much like a corpse that many said, "He's dead." But Jesus took him by the hand and lifted him to his feet, and he stood up.

MARK 9:19–27 NIV

Provision

The faithful love of the LORD never ends! His mercies never cease. Great is his faithfulness; his mercies begin afresh each morning. I say to myself, "The LORD is my inheritance; therefore, I will hope in him!" The LORD is good to those who depend on him, to those who search for him. So it is good to wait quietly for salvation from the LORD.

LAMENTATIONS 3:22–26 NLT

Portrait

In Christ, I have inherited God's promises (see 2 Peter 1:3–4).

MIND-RENEWING PRAYERS

DAY 1
Engrave Your Promises

I rise before the dawning of the morning, and cry for help;
I hope in Your word. My eyes are awake through the night watches,
that I may meditate on Your word.
PSALM 119:147–148 NKJV

Good morning, Lord. You are my Abba Father. Your Word has become my beacon. It is my light—day and night. It is my guidebook for raising my children and my faith. Engrave Your promises upon my heart. Make them part of every breath I take. Awaken me each day to Your good news!

Day 2
You Alone

But if any of you lacks wisdom, let him ask of God, who gives to
all generously and without reproach, and it will be given to him.
But he must ask in faith without any doubting, for the one who
doubts is like the surf of the sea, driven and tossed by the wind.
JAMES 1:5–6 NASB

My mind is running in a thousand different directions. I need Your wisdom,
Lord. Tell me what to do! Rid me of my doubts, for I am so tired of being
tossed around. This is no way to live. Calm my inner tumult. Remind me of
past blessings. Whisper Your Word in my ear. Encompass me with Your peace.
You alone I trust.

Day 3
Standing Strong

Fear ye not, stand still, and see the salvation of the LORD, which he will shew to
you to day: for the Egyptians whom ye have seen to day, ye shall see them again
no more for ever. The LORD shall fight for you, and ye shall hold your peace.
EXODUS 14:13–14 KJV

Sometimes, Lord, I am overly fearful for my children. Although I cannot hold
them in my arms of protection twenty-four hours a day, You can. So I refuse
to give in to fear. Instead, I place them in Your care. I stand strong in my faith
that You will fight for them. In doing so, I am left in Your peace, assured of
their safety and Your love.

Day 4
No Worries

Commit thy way unto the LORD; trust also in him; and he shall bring it to pass.
And he shall bring forth thy righteousness as the light, and thy judgment
as the noonday. Rest in the LORD, and wait patiently for him: fret not.
PSALM 37:5–7 KJV

Lord, I want to be like the Shunammite woman, knowing that no matter what happens to me or my children, with You in my life, all will be well. When I commit my life to You, when I trust and believe in Your promises, You bring them to fruition. So I am resting in You where I am safe, loved, protected, worry-free, and cared for.

Day 5
Limitless Love

I cried out, "I am slipping!" but your unfailing love, O LORD, supported me.
When doubts filled my mind, your comfort gave me renewed hope and cheer.
PSALM 94:18–19 NLT

The ways of this world seem determined to trip me up, Lord. It seems as if it would be so easy just to park myself in despair. But I refuse to sit in ashes. Instead, I seek Your face. I reach out for Your limitless love. I ask for Your forgiveness and solace. Help me to be a better mother for the children You have put in my care. Give me new hope and joy!

DAY 6
Calm Waters

Remember your promise to me; it is my only hope.
Your promise revives me; it comforts me in all my troubles.
PSALM 119:49–50 NLT

Bad news seems to be swirling around us, Lord. It's hard to keep from getting sucked in. But You are my peace. You calm my waters. You give me breath. In Your Word, Your promises, I see the light of life. In Your love, I find the hope to break out of this eddy and dive into Your arms. Thank You for keeping me buoyed by Your good news!

DAY 7
Out of the Shadows

Yes, and the Lord will deliver me from every evil attack and will bring me safely into his heavenly Kingdom. All glory to God forever and ever! Amen.
2 TIMOTHY 4:18 NLT

I feel like a thermometer, Lord, going up and down with every change in the wind, weather, and ways of man. Get me out of that mind-bog, Lord. Lift me up—mind, body, spirit, and soul. Bring me and my children out of the shadows and into Your heavenly kingdom. Show us how to be Your light on earth—to Your glory.

CHAPTER 10
Challenges concerning Temptations

Said Mr. Great-heart, Let them that are most afraid, keep close to me.
So the fiend came on, and the conductor met it; but when it was just come to
him, it vanished to all their sights. Then remembered they what had been said
some time ago, "Resist the devil, and he will flee from you" (James 4:7).

JOHN BUNYAN, *THE PILGRIM'S PROGRESS: PART 2*

• • • • • • •

Among believers, there are some misconceptions about temptation. The first is that once we enter the life of faith, temptations and our yielding to them will cease. Another fallacy is that any temptation—whether we act on it or not—is itself a sin and that we are at fault for the suggestions of evil that entered our mind. Both myths inevitably lead us into not only condemnation but discouragement, the continuing of which can result, at last, in actual sin.

But what—or who—exactly is the source of our temptation? The sly serpent, the Father of Lies. As he once whispered to the Mother of All Living Things while she was still in the garden, he continues to whisper to us mothers today. It is *he* who tempts us to look to him, the world, or our flesh to meet our needs. In other words, he tempts us to act independently of God. Such temptation approaches us via three channels, cited by the apostle John when he warns us:

> *Don't love the world's ways. Don't love the world's goods. Love of the world squeezes out love for the Father. Practically everything that goes on in the world—wanting your own way, wanting everything for yourself, wanting to appear important—has nothing to do with the Father. It just isolates you from him. The world and all its wanting, wanting, wanting is on the way out—but whoever does what God wants is set for eternity. (1 John 2:15–17 MSG, emphasis added)*

In Genesis 3:6 (ᴀᴍᴘ) we see how the devil brought the first mother down in three easy steps, from the first to the last nail in the coffin of a life in harmony with God:

Step 1: "The woman saw that the tree was good (suitable, pleasant) for food."

"Wanting your own way," or giving in to the lust of the flesh, draws you away from God's way (see Galatians 5:16–17), destroying your dependence upon Him (see John 15:5).

Step 2: "The woman saw. . .it was delightful to look at."

"Wanting everything for yourself," or giving in to the lust of your eyes, draws you away from God's Word (see Matthew 16:24–26), lessening your confidence in Him (see John 15:7).

Step 3: "The woman saw. . .a tree to be desired in order to make one wise, she took of its fruit and ate; and she gave some also to her husband, and he ate."

"Wanting to appear important," or the pride of your own life, draws you away from the worship of God (see 1 Peter 5:5–11), destroying your obedience to Him (see John 15:8–10).

Notice that Satan's methods speak to our very weaknesses. His goal is to draw us away from and attempt to destroy our relationship with God. And when we entertain and then act on the temptations he sets before our eyes, like a shiny red apple, we find ourselves not only sinning but also dragging the husband—and ultimately the kids—right along with us!

When we want our own way no matter what the consequences, we have fallen away from what God wants for us. When we have a craving for material things and do everything in our power to get them, we are catering to the lust of our eyes alone, and our selfishness is imposed. And when we move to appear important in our own eyes, we are no longer bowing to the true God or seeking His direction and commands. Instead we are drawn away from praising Him and wind up praising ourselves.

But how do these temptations arrive on our doorstep? It happens when the devil subtly prompts us with such thoughts as these—and makes it seem as if they came up from someplace deep down inside of us:

- Your way: *You're the mother. Make them do it your way—no matter how much it may hurt them. You deserve their respect. If they won't give it—take it! Besides, they owe you—you're the one who carried them around inside for nine months.*
- Your self: *You would look so good in that dress. So what if spending money on it means Sam won't be able to go on that class trip? He'll get over it.*
- Your pride: *That new position may take you away from home more. But imagine how much prestige that will give you! Why, everyone— including family—will be looking up to you! And when your status rises, so does the whole family's. We'll all get a boost up.*

These are only a few sample thoughts the devil puts on the blank screen of your mind. There are a myriad of other types of thoughts that may appear, unique to you and you alone. The important thing to remember is *you* are not bad if you think these thoughts—for they are being whispered in your ear by the evil one. The trouble starts when these thoughts are not captured and handed over to Christ. Because once we start to entertain them and live with them for a while, before we know it, we're going down the wrong road—and taking those we love right down with us!

So what's a mom to do? Someone once said that in overcoming temptations, confidence is the first thing, confidence is the second thing, and confidence is the third thing. In other words, we cannot let the fact that we're facing temptation discourage us but must stand confident in our faith and its strength instead. When Joshua was about to enter the Promised Land and face many foes, God told him, "Be strong and of a good courage. . . . Be not afraid, neither be thou dismayed . . . Only be thou strong and very courageous" (Joshua 1:6, 9, 7 KJV). And Jesus reinforces this command: "Let not your heart be troubled, neither let it be afraid" (John 14:27 KJV).

Instead of being discouraged when you face temptations, turn away from them and look for *and expect* God to deliver you. Understand He might not do it when or in the way you expect, for He has told us, "My thoughts are not your thoughts, nor are your ways My ways" (Isaiah 55:8 NKJV). But know and understand that He will do it! Put your confidence on the believing side—God's side, the winning side! He has overcome the world!

In addition, be a steady and faithful prayer, as well as a student of God's Word. And by "student," we mean memorize some Bible verses that will defend you against the devil's ploys. As Jesus demonstrated in the desert, God's Word can not only feed our minds, souls, spirits, and hearts but also keep the devil at bay. Besides, if you are filling the screen of your mind with Bible verses about strength, faith, and power, there'll be less room for the devil to plant his poison seed.

And mothers, take heart. The severity and power of your temptations—no matter what channel Satan has used to reach you—may be the strongest proof that you are in the right place—dwelling in the land of promise you have sought. After all, when the Israelites first left Egypt, God took the former slaves the long way around the Philistines, "lest peradventure the people repent when they see war, and they return to Egypt" (Exodus 13:17 KJV). But later, when the Israelites had more faith in God, He allowed them to be involved in a few skirmishes while in the wilderness, perhaps to test their mettle. It was only when they were entering the Promised Land that the real battles began.

So if you are facing a myriad of temptations, some stronger than others, you can know, oddly enough, that you are headed in the right direction and that God will get you through.

Although we may encounter temptations, if we are wholly in God's camp—mind, body, spirit, and soul—we will abhor them. Thus, keep your eyes open and on God. Pay attention to the thoughts that are wending their way through your head. If any seem to be coming from the dark side, immediately capture them, give them to Christ—and *leave them there*! So make up your mind, now, today, whose camp you are living in, whose side you are on:

Now therefore fear the LORD, and serve him in sincerity and in truth: and put away the gods which your fathers served on the other side of the flood, and in Egypt; and serve ye the LORD. And if it seem evil unto you to serve

*the LORD, choose you this day whom ye will serve; whether the gods which
your fathers served that were on the other side of the flood, or the gods of
the Amorites, in whose land ye dwell: but as for me and my house, we
will serve the LORD. (Joshua 24:14–15 KJV)*

If you are looking to the things of this world to save you—chocolate or french fries,
a new dress or purse or shoes, prominence, riches, or fame—or to the worldlings
themselves, you have taken your eyes off God. You've strayed from your base camp
and entered a wilderness. So remember to choose the one who has overcome the
world, the one in whom you will have success and prosper in all things! Pull up
stakes and pitch your tent on God's side once again!

"We must then commit ourselves to the Lord for victory over our temptations,
as we committed ourselves at first for forgiveness," Smith writes. "And we must
leave ourselves just as utterly in His hands for one as for the other."

Also take heart at the words of William Butler Yeats, who writes, "Every conquering temptation represents a new fund of moral energy. Every trial endured and
weathered in the right spirit makes a soul nobler and stronger than it was before."

Remember that God is faithful. He's put up an EXIT sign just for you. And
you'll find that if your eyes are open and your mind clear, God will show you a way
to escape temptation—even when there seems to be no way (see 1 Corinthians
10:13). You need merely keep your focus, heart, thoughts, spirit, and soul on Him,
and your faith *in* Him. He—and He alone—is your confidence (see Psalm 71:5).

*Now to Him Who is able to keep you without stumbling or slipping or falling,
and to present [you] unblemished (blameless and faultless) before the presence
of His glory in triumphant joy and exultation [with unspeakable,
ecstatic delight]—To the one only God, our Savior through Jesus Christ our Lord,
be glory (splendor), majesty, might and dominion, and power and authority,
before all time and now and forever (unto all the ages of eternity).
Amen (so be it).*
JUDE 1:24–25 AMP

$\mathcal{P}$ATH MARKERS

. . . .

$\mathcal{P}$romise

No test or temptation that comes your way is beyond the course of what others have had to face. All you need to remember is that God will never let you down; he'll never let you be pushed past your limit; he'll always be there to help you come through it.

1 CORINTHIANS 10:13 MSG

$\mathcal{P}$roof

The Holy Spirit led Jesus into the desert, so that the devil could test him. After Jesus had gone without eating for forty days and nights, he was very hungry. Then the devil came to him and said, "If you are God's Son, tell these stones to turn into bread."

Jesus answered, "The Scriptures say: 'No one can live only on food. People need every word that God has spoken.' "

Next, the devil took Jesus to the holy city and had him stand on the highest part of the temple. The devil said, "If you are God's Son, jump off. The Scriptures say: 'God will give his angels orders about you. They will catch you in their arms, and you won't hurt your feet on the stones.' "

Jesus answered, "The Scriptures also say, 'Don't try to test the Lord your God!' "

Finally, the devil took Jesus up on a very high mountain and showed him all the kingdoms on earth and their power. The devil said to him, "I will give all this to you, if you will bow down and worship me."

Jesus answered, "Go away Satan! The Scriptures say: 'Worship the Lord your God and serve only him.' "

Then the devil left Jesus, and angels came to help him.

MATTHEW 4:1–11 CEV

Provision

He is the one who will rescue you from hunters' traps and from deadly plagues. He will cover you with his feathers, and under his wings you will find refuge. His truth is your shield and armor. You do not need to fear terrors of the night, arrows that fly during the day.

PSALM 91:3–5 GW

Portrait

In Christ, I am more than a conqueror (see Romans 8:37).

MIND-RENEWING PRAYERS

DAY 1
Lift the Cloud

"Because he has set his love upon Me, therefore I will deliver him; I will set him on high, because he has known My name. He shall call upon Me, and I will answer him; I will be with him in trouble; I will deliver him and honor him."
PSALM 91:14–15 NKJV

Lord, I love You more than anything else in life. My eyes are on You and You alone. I am crying out to You for help, deliverance, saving. Lift the cloud of darkness off my mind. Fill me with Your good Word, Your light, Your love. Be with me now, in this moment. Break the spell of temptation that has come over me.

Day 2
On Solid Ground

*"Be strong and courageous; do not be afraid nor dismayed before
the king of Assyria, nor before all the multitude that is with him;
for there are more with us than with him."*
2 Chronicles 32:7 nkjv

*Dear God, give me the strength and courage to fight this temptation. It seems
so powerful. It's got me swaying—and I don't want to fall on the wrong side
of the path. Keep me close to You. I know You are the most powerful force in
heaven and on earth. And in that I rely, hope, and trust. I know You will
not—You cannot—fail to keep my feet on Your solid ground!*

Day 3
A Way Out

Wait [expectantly] for the Lord, and He will rescue you.
Proverbs 20:22 amp

*I am trying to be so patient, Lord. I know You are helping me to grow my
faith. I know You always provide a way out. I know You are the light that leads
me to safety. Come soon, Lord. Come rescue me. And while I expectantly wait
for You, give me Your peace, Your strength, Your courage to stay on Your
course—for where I lead, my family follows.*

Day 4
First in Your Mind

Behold, all they that were incensed against thee shall be ashamed and confounded: they shall be as nothing; and they that strive with thee shall perish.
ISAIAH 41:11 KJV

Lord, You have said You will fight all my battles. What a relief! For I have been running out of energy. So now I put all this in Your hands. I'm done with it. I'm stepping back and allowing Your power to flow through me. Thank You for defending me, for keeping the well-being of me and my family first in Your mind.

Day 5
Rest in Your Silence

So for the sake of Christ, I am well pleased and take pleasure in infirmities, insults, hardships, persecutions, perplexities and distresses; for when I am weak [in human strength], then am I [truly] strong (able, powerful in divine strength).
2 CORINTHIANS 12:10 AMP

When I abide in You, I feel cocooned in Your love, power, and goodness. Within You, I come to completion; I become the person You have created me to be. This gives me the strength to stay on the path You have laid out for me—one filled with Your beauty, Your vision. My heart thanks You, Jesus, as I rest in Your silence, away from the power of any temptations.

DAY 6

Gird My Heart

"What does the LORD your God require of you? He requires only
that you fear the LORD your God, and live in a way that pleases him,
and love him and serve him with all your heart and soul."
DEUTERONOMY 10:12 NLT

I am up against it again, Lord. A myriad of temptations has come upon me—
old ones and new ones. I turn my thoughts over to Your Son, for Him to take
captive. And that is where I leave them! Help me to come back into Your light
where all dark thoughts fade away. I want to love and serve You—and You
alone. Gird my heart. Fill my soul. Show me where to serve.

DAY 7

Write upon My Mind

"These things I have spoken to you, that in Me you may have peace.
In the world you will have tribulation; but be of good cheer,
I have overcome the world."
JOHN 16:33 NKJV

Thank You for Your Word and the peace it produces. Write upon my mind
the verses that will defend me from the tempter. Engrave upon my heart the
wisdom of the ages. Plant within my soul the fact that I can have joy. Thank
You, Jesus, the Unconquerable, for saving me—and mine!

CHAPTER 11
Challenges concerning Failures

And now was Christiana and her boys, and Mercy, received of the Lord at the head of the way, and spoke kindly unto by Him. Then said they yet further unto Him, We are sorry for our sins, and beg of our Lord His pardon, and further information what we must do. I grant pardon, said He, by word and deed: by word, in the promise of forgiveness; by deed, in the way I obtained it.
JOHN BUNYAN, *THE PILGRIM'S PROGRESS: PART 2*

• • • • • • •

Having, in the previous chapter, covered the victory we have in Jesus, you may wonder why this chapter is about failures in the higher life. Although while hidden in Christ we can win the battle over temptation, we would be remiss if we did not admit that even saints do weaken at times in the face of enticements, for we are dealing with fact, not theory.

Yes, ladies, even mothers are not perfect. We do sometimes fall short of the standards God has set for us (see Romans 3:23)—we miss the mark, or sin. Upon her pathway to holiness, a mother in Christ may find herself surprised by temptation and falling into sin. When she, like the prodigal son, suddenly comes to her senses (see Luke 15:17), she may then be tempted to be discouraged and give everything up as lost or to cover up the sin completely. Either option is lethal to the mom who wants to grow and progress in her Christian life. For the only real pathway available is to face that fact that she has indeed sinned, confess it to God, and discover, if possible, the reason and the remedy. Our divine union with God requires *absolute* honesty with Him and with ourselves.

When we fail, we really have no cause for discouragement and giving up. We must recognize the fact that we are not talking about a *state* but a *walk* of life with Christ. Smith writes, "The highway of holiness is not a *place*, but a *way*." When we, followers of the Way, stumble *off* the path, we can immediately check ourselves and find our way back—though we must be aware of where we are, hour by hour, minute by minute. If we have turned off the path, we must *instantly* return to the route the Father has mapped out for us and trust Him more than ever!

Soon after entering the Promised Land, the children of Israel suffered a disastrous defeat against the city of Ai. They were so discouraged that "the heart of the people sank, all spirit knocked out of them" (Joshua 7:5 MSG). The New King James Version relates the account like this:

> *Therefore the hearts of the people melted and became like water. Then Joshua tore his clothes, and fell to the earth on his face before the ark of the LORD until evening, he and the elders of Israel; and they put dust on their heads. And Joshua said, "Alas, Lord GOD, why have You brought this people over the Jordan at all—to deliver us into the hand of the Amorites, to destroy us? Oh, that we had been content, and dwelt on the other side of the Jordan! O Lord, what shall I say when Israel turns its back before its enemies?" (Joshua 7:5–8)*

Talk about despair and discouragement! How many of us have felt as if we've had the spirit knocked out of us? How often have we felt our hearts melt and become like water? Have you ever cried out, "What made me ever think it would be a good idea to have kids? I must've been nuts. Would that I had not ventured into this territory"? By so saying, we are in despair about not only the present but the future as well. We become immobilized, not wanting to take another step backward or forward. Our discouragement leaves us in a sort of limbo, a place where there is no growth, no progress, no future. After such an overwhelming failure— emotionally, physically, mentally, spiritually—we may find it easier to wallow in our despondency, our faces on the ground and dust on our heads, than to look up to God. But God, as always, has a better idea. As He told Joshua, He tells us, "Get up!" (Joshua 7:10 NKJV).

But what keeps our heads down? Perhaps it is the thought that God will find it hard to forgive us. In fact, He may not forgive us at all! Or if He does, it may take Him days, perhaps years, to get over it. Hannah Whitall Smith writes about a conversation she had with a little girl who had trouble believing Jesus forgives us for our sins as soon as we ask Him:

> *"Well," [the child] said deliberately, "I cannot believe that. I should think He would make us feel sorry for two or three days first. And then I should think He would make us ask Him a great many times and in a very pretty way, too, not just in common talk. And I believe that is the way he does, and you need not try to make me think He forgives me right at once, no matter what the Bible says." She only said what most Christians think, and what is worse, what most Christians act on, making their discouragement and their very remorse separate them infinitely further off from God than their sin would have done. Yet it is so totally contrary to the way we like our children to act toward us that I wonder how we ever could have conceived such an idea of God. How a mother grieves when a naughty child goes off alone in despairing remorse and doubts her willingness to forgive; and how, on the other hand, her whole heart goes out in welcoming love to the repentant little one who runs to her at once and begs her forgiveness!*

Thank God that as soon as we come to Him and confess our sins, He forgives (see 1 John 1:9 KJV)! Immediately! There is no silent treatment, no grudge. *And this we must believe!* For if we do not, we have made God out to be a liar (see 1 John 5:10).

As soon as consciousness of our sin has set in, we must immediately lift up our faces to God and become conscious of His forgiveness. We can only continue walking on this path of holiness by taking our eyes off our misstep and "looking unto Jesus" (Hebrews 12:2 KJV). Otherwise, we will keep tripping up!

Once our eyes are back on Him, we can confess what we have done. Within that confession may lie our motives. When Achan confessed to Joshua, he said:

> *"Indeed I have sinned against the LORD God of Israel, and this is what I have done: When I saw among the spoils a beautiful Babylonian garment, two hundred shekels of silver, and a wedge of gold weighing fifty shekels, I coveted them and took them. And there they are, hidden in the earth in the midst of my tent, with the silver under it." (Joshua 7:20–21 NKJV)*

Do you see Achan's path to sin here? He saw, coveted, took, then hid. In four steps, Achan, who had taken his eyes off God, had intentionally sinned. Does this progression sound somewhat familiar? Eve did the same thing in the garden. She saw the fruit that would make her wise. She coveted it then took it. Later she hid from God.

A woman who did not follow this pattern was Salome, the New Testament mother of James and John, the sons of Zebedee. In a moment of zealous ambition for her sons, she bowed before Jesus and, probably at her sons' bidding, asked Him a favor:

> *"Give your word that these two sons of mine will be awarded the highest places of honor in your kingdom, one at your right hand, one at your left hand."*
>
> *Jesus responded, "You have no idea what you're asking." And he said to James and John, "Are you capable of drinking the cup that I'm about to drink?"*
>
> *They said, "Sure, why not?"*
>
> *Jesus said, "Come to think of it, you are going to drink my cup. But as to awarding places of honor, that's not my business. My Father is taking care of that."*

When the ten others heard about this, they lost their tempers, thoroughly disgusted with the two brothers. So Jesus got them together to settle things down. He said, "You've observed how godless rulers throw their weight around, how quickly a little power goes to their heads. It's not going to be that way with you. Whoever wants to be great must become a servant. Whoever wants to be first among you must be your slave. That is what the Son of Man has done: He came to serve, not be served." (Matthew 20:21–28 MSG)

Salome must have been not only disappointed in Jesus' answer to her request but, after hearing His admonishment, somewhat embarrassed as well. It's interesting that she had put on this pretense of humbleness prior to asking for something that served her (and her children's) ambition—but not God! She, like Eve, wanted her own way (not God's will), wanted everything for her children (instead of for God), and wanted her boys to appear important (drawing them *and herself* away from God).

Yet, kudos to her, in one respect she did not follow in the footsteps of Eve: Salome did not hide after her request. She took Jesus' admonishment on the chin. She learned where she'd made her mistake and what the root cause had been and gleaned Jesus' wisdom. Then, like her sons, she continued to follow Him. Salome was present at His crucifixion, where Jesus asked her son John to take care of His mother, Mary, and she was at Jesus' tomb during His resurrection.

When we have sinned, we need to acknowledge it. We, like the children of Israel, must rise "early in the morning" (Joshua 7:16 KJV), then run to where our sins are hidden, take them from the midst of their hiding places, and lay them before the Lord (see Joshua 7:22–23). At that point, we can stone them, burn them, and bury them (see Joshua 7:25–26) and immediately receive God's forgiveness, encouragement, and victory, as did Joshua and the Israelites. "Do not be afraid, nor be dismayed; take all the people of war with you, and arise, go up to Ai. See, I have given into your hand the king of Ai, his people, his city, and his land" (Joshua 8:1 NKJV).

If we do not confess our sins, even some innocent or seemingly harmless habits or indulgences, and continue to attempt to hide them from God (an insane endeavor since *He sees and knows everything*), not only do we distance ourselves from God but our misdeeds will also take on a snowball effect until we (and perhaps our family members) are buried by them. (See King David's story beginning in 2 Samuel 11 where his sin with Bathsheba gets the proverbial snowball rolling.) Or we will end up like Peter—who three times refused to admit to knowing Jesus, resulting in denials, anger at others, and cursing and swearing—and find ourselves weeping bitter tears (see Matthew 26:69–75).

Confessing sins is not really for God's benefit because He already knows what we've done. It is more for our own benefit and growth. For when we admit a sin or indulgence, we are bringing it into the light, enabling us to forgive ourselves for the deed done in the past, to request God's help in finding its cause in the present, and to help guard against it in the future.

Let's make the following words our continual plea before God: "Investigate my life, O God, find out everything about me; cross-examine and test me, get a clear picture of what I'm about; see for yourself whether I've done anything wrong— then guide me on the road to eternal life" (Psalm 139:23–24 MSG). If we do so, we will be living not only right but light!

For once you were full of darkness, but now you have
light from the Lord. So live as people of light!
EPHESIANS 5:8 NLT

 Path Markers

Promise

If we confess our sins, He is faithful and righteous to forgive us our sins and to cleanse us from all unrighteousness.

1 John 1:9 NASB

Proof

Oh, what joy for those whose disobedience is forgiven, whose sin is put out of sight! Yes, what joy for those whose record the Lord has cleared of guilt, whose lives are lived in complete honesty! When I refused to confess my sin, my body wasted away, and I groaned all day long. Day and night your hand of discipline was heavy on me. My strength evaporated like water in the summer heat. . . . Finally, I confessed all my sins to you and stopped trying to hide my guilt.

I said to myself, "I will confess my rebellion to the Lord." And you forgave me! All my guilt is gone.

Psalm 32:1–5 NLT

Provision

Who is a God like you, who pardons sin and forgives the transgression of the remnant of his inheritance? You do not stay angry forever but delight to show mercy. You will again have compassion on us; you will tread our sins underfoot and hurl all our iniquities into the depths of the sea.

Micah 7:18–19 TNIV

Portrait

In Christ, I am not only redeemed but forgiven (see Ephesians 1:7).

DAY 1

A Multitude of Mercies

Have mercy upon me, O God, according to Your lovingkindness;
according to the multitude of Your tender mercies, blot out my transgressions.
Wash me thoroughly from my iniquity, and cleanse me from my sin.
PSALM 51:1–2 NKJV

Lord, I definitely need a "multitude of Your tender mercies" because I made
a big mistake and it really snowballed out of control. In fact, at this point,
it's more like an avalanche. What kind of example am I to my kids—and
the rest of the world? Forgive me, Lord. And give me the courage to ask my
children for forgiveness as well.

DAY 2

At My Doorstep

For I acknowledge my transgressions, and my sin is always before me.
Against You, You only, have I sinned, and done this evil in Your sight—
that You may be found just when You speak, and blameless when You judge.
PSALM 51:3–4 NKJV

Jesus, I cannot run from this wrong that is lying at my doorstep. Nor can I hide
from its effects on me and the rest of my family. Give me the courage to put into
words what You need to hear. Help me to forgive myself as well. And give me
insight as to the root of this sin. For I'd rather not come this way again.

Day 3
Love No Matter What

Behold, You desire truth in the inward parts,
and in the hidden part You will make me to know wisdom.
PSALM 51:6 NKJV

Deep, deep down, God, I know I must face the truth. My sin, my lie seems ugly
to look at right now, but I must not hide it any longer. The only thing giving
me the power to face my failure is the knowledge that You will love me—no
matter what. As I love my children, You love me. As easily as I forgive them,
forgive me.

Day 4
Stick with Me, Lord!

Create in me a clean heart, O God, and renew a steadfast spirit within me.
Do not cast me away from Your presence, and do not take Your Holy Spirit
from me. Restore to me the joy of Your salvation,
and uphold me by Your generous Spirit.
PSALM 51:10–12 NKJV

I don't feel very clean today, Lord. In fact, I feel just the opposite. But I know
You have the power to power-wash my heart. Only You can make me feel new
again. Stick with me, Lord, in spite of what I've done. Give me back the joy I
once had. Lift me out of the dark abyss and into the light of Your love and life.

Day 5
At This Very Moment

As far as the east is from the west,
so far has He removed
our transgressions from us.
PSALM 103:12 NKJV

There are so many things I need to confess to You, Lord. Things I have been ignoring. But they must come out now, today, at this very moment! By not telling You everything, I have become unhappy with myself. And this is being reflected in my behavior and my attitude toward my family. So forgive me, Lord. Move me so far from my sins that I never see them again!

Day 6
Guide Me Back

Search me, O God, and know my heart; test me and know
my anxious thoughts. Point out anything in me that offends you,
and lead me along the path of everlasting life.
PSALM 139:23–24 NLT

I'm feeling restless and anxious, Lord. And I think it's because I've buried some things, some wrongs—in attitude, judgments, selfishness, whatever— so deep, and now I am suffering the painful consequences. Search me now, Lord. Gently show me what I have hidden within that I need to release. Guide me back on the path to You.

Day 7

Focused on the Light

Let us run with patience the race that
is set before us, looking unto Jesus.
HEBREWS 12:1–2 KJV

I refuse to let my past sins trip me up. Instead, I am putting my faith and feet to
the path that leads to You. My eyes are on You and You alone. Help me to run
this race You have laid before me. Help me put the darkness of yesterdays behind
me and keep focused on the light of the present. Today and forever. Amen.

CHAPTER 12
Challenges concerning Perspective

[Christiana's son] Matthew: I think God has been wonderful good
unto us, both in bringing us out of this Valley, and in delivering us
out of the hand of this enemy; for my part, I see no reason, why we
should distrust our God any more, since He has now, and in such
a place as this, given us such testimony of His love as this.
JOHN BUNYAN, *THE PILGRIM'S PROGRESS: PART 2*

• • • • • • •

One of the greatest challenges facing Christians, especially moms, is seeing that everything—good and bad—comes from God's hand. Hannah Whitall Smith writes:

People say, "I can easily submit to things that come from God; but I
cannot submit to man, and most of my trials and crosses come through
human instrumentality." Or they say, "It is all well enough to talk of
trusting; but when I commit a matter to God, man is sure to come in
and disarrange it all; and while I have no difficulty in trusting God,
I do see serious difficulties in the way of trusting men."

Almost everything we encounter in our lives comes to us through human instrumentalities, and so most of our trials are the result of some man or woman's failure, ignorance, carelessness, cruelty, or sin. But how could an all-loving God put mothers through heartbreaks, especially where it concerns our children? How can we pray, "Thy will be done"?

Again, Smith writes:

What good is there in trusting our affairs to God, if, after all, man is to be allowed to come in and disarrange them; and how is it possible to live by faith, if human agencies, in which it would be wrong and foolish to trust, are to have a prevailing influence in moulding our lives? . . .

What is needed, then, is to see God in everything and to receive everything directly from His hands with no intervention of second causes. And it is to this that we must be brought before we can know an abiding experience of entire abandonment and perfect trust. Our abandonment must be to God, not to man. And our trust must be in Him, not in any arm of flesh, or we shall fail at the first trial.

Scripture supports Smith's claim that there are no "second causes" for the believing Christian—that everything comes to us through our Father's hand and with His knowledge, no matter what person or circumstances may have been the apparent agents. Here are the facts:

- God knows exactly how many hairs are on our head (see Luke 12:7).
- God knows what we need before we even ask (see Matthew 6:32).
- God avenges those who wrong us (see Romans 12:19).
- God is not only on our side but will fight our battles for us (see 2 Chronicles 20:17).
- God is for us, so no one can stand against us (see Romans 8:31).
- God is our shepherd, so we are never in need (see Psalm 23:1).
- God is by our side when we pass through the waters and the fire (see Isaiah 43:2).
- God, our divine helper, will neither leave us nor forsake us (see Hebrews 13:5-6).
- God delivers and rescues us (see Daniel 6:27).
- God holds the hearts of kings in His hands (see Proverbs 21:1).
- God controls the wind and the waves (see Mark 4:39).

Because second causes are under the management of our Father, not one of them can reach us without God's permission and knowledge. Everything (except our own sinfulness) comes from our Lord. "It may be the sin of man that originates the action, and therefore the thing itself cannot be said to be the will of God," Smith writes, "but by the time it reaches us, it has become God's will for us and must be accepted as coming directly from His hands."

Here's an illustration that may help us. When a mother holds her child in her arms, she is very protective, for she knows her little one is basically helpless. Nothing can touch that child without its mom's permission, unless she is too weak to defend it. Yet even if this is the case, the mother will suffer the harm in herself first before she allows it to reach her babe. If this is how it is with an earthly mother, imagine how it is with a spiritual Father who encircles us with an unfathomable amount of love, care, and presence! Smith writes, "Nothing can disturb or harm us, except He shall see that it is best for us, and shall stand aside to let it pass." Everything that touches us goes through God first. We must realize that *no evil exists—no matter how dark and bleak—that God cannot turn into good*.

Thus through every blessing as well as every trial, we must be patient and totally abandoned to God's will and way, to His plan for us *and* our children. Remember that God loved His Son, Jesus, as much on the cross at Calvary as He did on Mount Tabor, where Jesus was transfigured.

Remember Joseph of the Old Testament? His brothers sold him to some merchants, after which he served as a slave, was accused of rape, and was thrown into a dungeon. Following these hardships, Joseph miraculously became the number two man in Egypt, which enabled him later to save the lives of his father and his brothers and their families. He told his siblings:

> *Don't be sad or angry with yourselves that you sold me. . . . God sent me ahead of you to make sure that you would have descendants on the earth and to save your lives in an amazing way. It wasn't you who sent me here, but God. . . . Even though you planned evil against me, God planned good to come out of it. (Genesis 45:5, 7–8; 50:20 GW)*

Through all his trials and successes, our Father God was with Joseph—and Joseph stayed with Him (see Genesis 39:20–21, 23). Because Joseph remained close to the Lord, our Creator God turned Joseph's trials into a blessing—not only for Joseph himself but for the sons of Israel! And God promises to do the same for us!

God is not the author of sin, but He uses His creativity and His wisdom to work the design of His providence to His—and our—advantage. All we need to do is trust Him to work things out to our good. He will overrule events, trials, and tragedies in our lives to His glory and our praise!

Being women, we often try to fix things—for ourselves and our kids—and get frustrated when we can't. Moms, those are times when we need to let go and let God. Because *He* is the "Great Fixer." Oftentimes He sees solutions we cannot even imagine! After all, He is the *Creator* God. As the great I Aм, He has everything under His power. Are you allowing God to work in the events of your life—or are you too busy "fixing them" to let Him into the situations, thus blocking His way?

Let's look at some biblical women who thought God needed some help in "fixing" certain situations. There was Sarah, who told her husband, Abraham, to sleep with her maid Hagar so that God's promise of a son for Abraham would come to fruition. The result? The eternal feud between half brothers Ishmael and Isaac.

Then there was Rebekah, who fixed things so that her favored son, Jacob, would receive her husband, Isaac's, blessing and have everything she'd dreamed of him having. The result? The older brother, Esau, threatened Jacob's life *and* Rebekah never saw her beloved Jacob again.

Then there was the impatient Rachel, Jacob's favorite wife, who was barren. She became jealous of all the sons her sister, Leah, was giving Jacob. So she demanded of him, "Give me sons or I'll die!" (Genesis 30:1 мsg). The results? Rachel did eventually give birth to two sons but died bringing the second into the world.

And then there are the cursers, like Job's wife. After Job and his wife lost everything they had, including their children, she advised him to "curse God and die." But Job, the wiser of the two, responded with, "You talk like a foolish woman. Should we accept only good things from the hand of God and never anything bad?" (Job 2:9–10 nlt).

In contrast to these fixers, demanders, and cursers was Leah. Although the less loved of Jacob's wives (Rachel being the favored), she bore him six sons and daughter Dinah. Of those six sons, Judah became the ancestor of David and Jesus, and Levi became the forerunner of God's priests. Unlike her sister, Rachel, Leah seemed to have found contentment in the midst of her many trials, for the Bible records neither complaint nor envy from the plainer sister.

Like Dorothy in *The Wizard of Oz*, we sometimes have to go quite a distance down that long, yellow-brick road of loss, grief, tragedy, and trials before we find our way home. But we *will* get there—as will our children, although it may break our hearts to see them suffer! Yet the amazing thing about this is that many times while we are walking, we have incredible life-changing experiences and learn valuable lessons along the way.

Our God is an awesome God! He leads us through desert places. But if we keep our eyes on His pillar of light and follow the cloud He sends before us, He will continue to take care of us and will one day lead us to the Promised Land (see Genesis 50:24–25).

Our part is to trust that everything we experience—good or bad—comes through Him to us. We are not to be beguiled by the darkness of doubts, what-ifs, supposes, and trials but to understand that He is with us in the midst of our storms and will find an awesomely creative way to turn whatever evil confronts us into our eventual good.

We need not enjoy our trials but simply understand that we must trust God's will, wisdom, and creativity in the midst of them and impress the certainty upon our minds that He is with us through it all until the end of the age (see Matthew 28:20). Knowing this, we can simply let go with abandon and let God work His wonders in good times and bad, praising Him all the way.

I live and breathe God; if things aren't going well, hear this and be happy. . . .
God is listening, ready to rescue you. If your heart is broken, you'll find God
right there; if you're kicked in the gut, he'll help you catch your breath.
Disciples so often get into trouble; still, God is there every time.
PSALM 34:2, 17–19 MSG

Promise

The moment we get tired in the waiting, God's Spirit is right alongside helping us along. If we don't know how or what to pray, it doesn't matter. He does our praying in and for us, making prayer out of our wordless sighs, our aching groans. He knows us far better than we know ourselves, knows our pregnant condition, and keeps us present before God. That's why we can be so sure that every detail in our lives of love for God is worked into something good.

ROMANS 8:26–28 MSG

Proof

[Nebuchadnezzar] commanded the most mighty men that were in his army to bind Shadrach, Meshach, and Abednego, and to cast them into the burning fiery furnace. Then these men were bound in their coats, their hosen, and their hats, and their other garments, and were cast into the midst of the burning fiery furnace. . . .

Then Nebuchadnezzar the king was astonished, and rose up in haste, and spake, and said unto his counsellors, Did not we cast three men bound into the midst of the fire? They answered and said unto the king, True, O king.

He answered and said, Lo, I see four men loose, walking in the midst of the fire, and they have no hurt; and the form of the fourth is like the Son of God. Then Nebuchadnezzar came near to the mouth of the burning fiery furnace, and spake, and said, Shadrach, Meshach, and Abednego, ye servants of the most high God, come forth, and come hither. Then Shadrach, Meshach, and Abednego, came forth of the midst of the fire. And the princes, governors, and captains, and the king's counsellors, being gathered together, saw these men, upon whose bodies the fire had no power, nor was an hair of their head singed, neither were their coats changed, nor the smell of fire had passed on them.

Then Nebuchadnezzar spake, and said, Blessed be the God of Shadrach,

Meshach, and Abednego, who hath sent his angel, and delivered his servants that trusted in him, and have changed the king's word, and yielded their bodies, that they might not serve nor worship any god, except their own God.

DANIEL 3:20–21, 24–28 KJV

Provision

Praise God, the Father of our Lord Jesus Christ! The Father is a merciful God, who always gives us comfort. He comforts us when we are in trouble, so that we can share that same comfort with others in trouble.

2 CORINTHIANS 1:3–4 CEV

Portrait

I am assured of God's presence in any and all situations (see Isaiah 43:2).

MIND-RENEWING PRAYERS

DAY 1
Flood and Fire

"When you pass through the waters, I will be with you; and through the rivers, they shall not overflow you. When you walk through the fire, you shall not be burned, nor shall the flame scorch you."

ISAIAH 43:2 NKJV

I feel as if I'm drowning, Lord. My grief, my loss, my sorrow are overwhelming. But You have promised to be with me through flood and fire. So I'm reaching out to You right now. Pull me up out of these tumultuous waves. Heal my heart. Pour Your love and mercy down upon me. I'm looking to You—my one and only sure hope.

DAY 2
Something Good

The LORD is on my side; I will not fear.
What can man do to me?
PSALM 118:6 NKJV

I know You are on my side, God. I know that with You, I can be brave. I can ignore what people attempt to do to me. But when people mess with my kids, it's a different story. Help me to keep them in Your loving care—for I feel helpless to defend them. I am picturing them—and myself—safe in Your arms. Hold us tight! Don't ever let us go! Turn this into something good!

DAY 3
Lord of Peace and Love

"Give your entire attention to what God is doing right now,
and don't get worked up about what may or may not happen tomorrow.
God will help you deal with whatever hard things come up when the time comes."
MATTHEW 6:34 MSG

My mind is running rampant with what-ifs, maybes, and supposes, especially when it comes to my child. These thoughts are keeping me up at night! But You are the Lord of peace and love. So help me just to keep my eyes on You and myself in You. Help me focus on today and leave tomorrow in Your hands.

DAY 4
Dear Shelter

*They should seek the Lord, if haply they might feel after him,
and find him, though he be not far from every one of us:
for in him we live, and move, and have our being.*
ACTS 17:27–28 KJV

*I feel Your presence, Father God. You are surrounding my entire being with
Your light and love. With You and You alone do I feel safe. You are my mighty
rock and fortress. You are my saving grace. You have the wings under which I
take refuge. In You I live and move and am. My dear shelter from all storms,
comfort me. Tell me all is well.*

DAY 5
In Your Wisdom

*"What's the price of a pet canary? Some loose change, right? And God cares
what happens to it even more than you do. He pays even greater attention to
you, down to the last detail—even numbering the hairs on your head!"*
MATTHEW 10:29–30 MSG

*Wow! You know every little detail about the world I live in and everything
about me. So you know what's happening in my life right now. Lord, I know
that in Your wisdom You will make things turn out all right someday. In the
meantime, I need Your help. Lavish upon me the love and comfort I need to
get through this day.*

DAY 6

More Like Leah

*While Joseph was in prison, the LORD was with him. The LORD reached
out to him with his unchanging love and gave him protection. . . .
The LORD was with Joseph and made whatever he did successful.*
GENESIS 39:20–21, 23 GW

Lord, no matter what is going on in my life, I know You are with me. So help
me to be more like Leah and Joseph. Help me to be content in my present
situation. Help me to remember that I can't help what people around me
do, but I can control how I respond. Give me patience. Give me love. Make
something good come out of all this, beginning with me.

DAY 7

Until This Passes

*We can rejoice, too, when we run into problems and trials, for we know that
they help us develop endurance. And endurance develops strength of character,
and character strengthens our confident hope of salvation.*
ROMANS 5:3–4 NLT

I want to rejoice, Lord, but I am finding it very difficult to do so right now.
You know what is happening in my life. And I know You want to turn this to
good. In the meantime, help me to be strong. Give me hope. Fill me with Your
peace. Hold me until this passes, until these growing pains are over, and I can
smile again.

PART 3:

Results

Praise the Lord! . . . We escaped like a
bird from a hunter's trap. The trap is broken,
and we are free! Our help is from the Lord,
who made heaven and earth.

PSALM 124:6–8 NLT

Chapter 13

Slave Girl or Freewoman

[Great Heart said,] Sin has delivered us up to the just curse of a righteous law; now, from this curse we must be justified by way of redemption, a price being paid for the harms we have done (Romans 4:24); and this is by the blood of your Lord, who came and stood in your place and stead, and died your death for your transgressions (Galatians 3:13).
John Bunyan, *The Pilgrim's Progress: Part 2*

• • • • • • •

Although we are grown women with children of our own, no matter *how* old we get, we will never stop being the children of God. And as His children, we can choose to live in one of two ways: as a slave girl or a freewoman.

As a slave, the mother's soul is controlled by an unwavering obligation to obey the laws of God, either because the poor thing fears God will punish her *or* because she expects some kind of payment for the duties she performs. As a freewoman, the controlling authority is a new *inner* woman who works out the will of the divine Creator without fear of being punished or expectation of reward. In the first scenario, the Christian mother is bound in servitude, walking in the flesh, knocking herself out, hoping her actions will please her overseer. In the second, she is free in and redeemed by Christ, a daughter of the King, an heir to His promises, walking in the Spirit, and working simply for love of her God.

The true pathway, of course, is that of the freewoman. But sadly, once we have started out on our walks, we are often led astray, falling back into our former lives of bondage to the world. Yet this is nothing new, for it happened in the early church. In his letter to the Galatians, the apostle Paul addressed the fact that some Jewish believers there were insisting Gentile believers obey the ceremonies and rites of Jewish law. On one occasion, even Peter, in an attempt to please men instead of God, and Barnabas sided with these legalistic Jews called Judaizers (see Galatians 2:12–13)!

Apparently, even the most dedicated Christians can fall back into bondage by stumbling off the true path. But Paul, who had confronted Peter, now set his readers straight, telling them, "We know that a person is made right with God not by *following the law*, but by *trusting in Jesus Christ*" (Galatians 2:16 NCV, emphasis added).

Thus, we are saved through our *faith* in Christ and Christ alone. Anything we *add* to that formula is not of God and puts us in bondage. The Judaizers added ceremonial law. We add religious routines and our own egos (glorifying ourselves instead of God). Sometimes we add our Christian works—teaching Sunday school, serving on the church board, signing up for nursery duty, and so forth. Not that there is anything *wrong* with these tasks. The problem comes when we begin substituting our works for faith. But get this straight in your mind: God is not so much interested in what you *do* as He is in what you *are*. God has His eye on your inner woman, the new creature born when you first accepted Christ.

In Galatians 4:24–31, Paul presents an analogy to help us understand we are freewomen and not slaves. It's the story of Abraham who had two sons—the first by Hagar, his wife's slave, and the second by Sarah, his wife. In Paul's analogy, Hagar represents the law while Sarah represents God's grace. Ishmael, Hagar's son, was born as a result of human conniving. Isaac, Sarah's son, was born as a result of God's good promise. "The two births represent two ways of being in relationship with God" (Galatians 4:24 MSG). As spiritually reborn children of God's promise, freedwomen cannot go back to lives of slavery under the law—because law (the son of the slave woman) and grace (the son of the freewoman) cannot exist together!

To help you understand the difference between the bondage of the law and the freedom-filled Gospel of Christ and to perhaps discover where your own bondage or freedom lies, here are a few comparisons (emphasis added):

- The Law says, "*Do* this and you will live" (Luke 10:28 NASB).

The Gospel says, "*Live* and then you will do" (see Galatians 5:16–18).

- The Law says, "*Make* yourselves a new heart and a new spirit!" (Ezekiel 18:31 NASB).

  The Gospel says, "I will *give* you a new heart and put a new spirit within you" (Ezekiel 36:26 NASB).

- The Law says, "*You must love* the LORD your God with all your heart, all your soul, and all your strength" (Deuteronomy 6:5 NLT).

  The Gospel says, "This is real love—not that we loved God, but that *he loved us* and sent his Son as a sacrifice to take away our sins" (1 John 4:10 NLT).

- The Law says, "The *wages* of sin is death" (Romans 6:23 NKJV).

  The Gospel says, "The *gift* of God is eternal life in Christ Jesus our Lord" (Romans 6:23 NKJV).

- The Law says, "You *must be* holy" (Leviticus 20:26 NIrV).

  The Gospel says, "Christ's death has *made* you holy" (Colossians 1:22 NIrV).

- The Law says, "Blessings are the result of *obedience*" (see Deuteronomy 11:27).

  The Gospel says, "Obedience is the result of *blessings*" (see James 1:25).

- The Law says, "Do these things" (Numbers 15:13 NASB).

  The Gospel says, "Everything is done!" (John 19:30 CEV).

In *What God Wishes Christians Knew about Christianity*, Bill Gillham writes:

God describes Christ as our internal *control center in Romans 8:2: "For the law of the spirit of life in Christ Jesus has set you free from the law of sin and of death." You can identify His law of love within you—it's* an inner urging, a longing, a strong sensing, a desire *to live in a manner that is pleasing to God. That's the Spirit of Christ in you, and it beats the daylight out of living under a hard taskmaster who continually badgers you with "you* ought *to, you* must, *you* should, *you* have *to,"* etc. Law has no life *in it. It "ministers" condemnation (2 Corinthians 3:6, 9).*

God's law had a purpose—to tell us where we were falling short (see Galatians 3:24–25). And although it served to bring us to Christ (see Galatians 3:24–25), it can never save us. Only Christ can do that.

Because there was no way we could satisfy the demands of the Law of Moses, God, through Jesus, gave us two new laws to replace all others: " 'Love the Lord your God with all your heart, with all your soul, and with all your mind.' This is the greatest and most important commandment. The second is like it: 'Love your neighbor as you love yourself' " (Matthew 22:37–39 GW).

When we attempt to live in accordance with the law, we become severed from Christ. We find ourselves "fallen away from grace (from God's gracious favor and unmerited blessing)" (Galatians 5:4 AMP). Yet *we are no longer under the Law of Moses but under the law of Christ*—to love God and each other. As we obey this law in Christ, we find ourselves walking not in the flesh but in the spirit! Smith writes:

Legal Christians do not deny Christ; they only seek to add something to Christ. Their idea is, Christ—and something besides. Perhaps it is Christ and good works, or Christ and earnest feelings, or Christ and clear doctrines, or Christ and certain religious performances. All these are good in themselves and good as the results or fruits of salvation; but to add anything to Christ, no matter how good it may be, as the procuring cause of salvation, is to deny His completeness and to exalt self.

It may not be law that you have added to Christ but a certain ritual you believe will please others. Or it may be some work of which you are very proud (thus glorifying your own ego). Smith writes, "A religion of bondage always exalts self. It is what I do—*my* efforts, *my* wrestlings, *my* faithfulness" (emphasis in original).

Moms, we are in bondage if what we hope to see in the eyes of others—including our children—is our own reflection. Better that we be freedwomen, looking to leave the reflection of Christ in the eyes of all.

Regardless of whether we women are slaves or free, we all have one thing in common: children with big ears and eyes, always listening to what we say and watching what we do. In most cases, our children are likely to repeat our behavior. So the question is, are we showing them how to live in bondage to laws and empty rituals or how to live in the freedom of Christ?

The secret is to be as God sees us—*as little children ourselves*. "You are no longer slaves but God's children. Since you are God's children, God has also *made* you heirs" (Galatians 4:7 GW, emphasis added). Notice the past tense—"made"! You are *already* an heir. It's a done deal! Get God's view of you set in your mind. Walk as if you are the daughter of the King that you are! Because "unless you change and become like little children, you will never enter the kingdom of heaven" (Matthew 18:3 GW). Smith writes:

> *It is impossible to get the child-spirit until the servant-spirit has disappeared. Notice, I do not say the spirit of service, but the servant-spirit. Every good child is filled with the spirit of service but ought not to have anything of the servant-spirit. The child serves from love; the servant works for wages.*

Your young children don't need to struggle to survive. They don't need to earn or carry around their own money—for you provide for them. You feed, clothe, shelter, and love the heirs of your own little kingdom. That's the way God cares for us. He not only provides everything we need but also gives us blessings besides. We need not worry, stress, or strain about the future. We need not become desperate for riches other than the ones He provides in Christ. We need not try to please anyone except Him—not our children, our bosses, our husbands, or ourselves—but only to serve God with great love and affection. He is not a hard master (see Matthew

25:24) but an affectionate and loving Father.

Because God has sacrificed His Son, as God's heir you can "stride freely through wide open spaces" (Psalm 119:45 MSG), unfettered by the opinions of others—*including yourself*. You are God's willing servant, not a slave. And because He works in you "[energizing and creating in you the power and desire], both to will and to work for His good pleasure and satisfaction and delight" (Philippians 2:13 AMP), all you need to do is accept God as your Father, become as a little child, and allow Him to take over your life—to put Him in the driver's seat.

As God's daughter of the promises, having put aside all self-effort and self-dependence, you will receive "the unending (boundless, fathomless, incalculable, and exhaustless) riches of Christ [wealth which no human being could have searched out]" (Ephesians 3:8 AMP).

So relax. Stop battling to win God over. You already have! Rest in Daddy God. Recognize that you are His child, a beautiful daughter and heir, a freewoman, a new creature in Christ. Allow His Spirit to have His way. Sit back and leave the driving to Him. And let the fun—and joy—begin!

If you abide in My word [hold fast to My teachings and live
in accordance with them], you are truly My disciples.
And you will know the Truth, and the Truth will set you free.
JOHN 8:31–32 AMP

Path Markers
....

Promise

A new heart will I give you and a new spirit will I put within you.

EZEKIEL 36:26 AMP

Proof

For Christ's love compels us, because we are convinced that one died for all, and therefore all died. And he died for all, that those who live should no longer live for themselves but for him who died for them and was raised again. So from now on we regard no one from a worldly point of view. Though we once regarded Christ in this way, we do so no longer. Therefore, if anyone is in Christ, the new creation has come: The old has gone, the new is here!

2 CORINTHIANS 5:14–17 NIV

Provision

It is God Who is all the while effectually at work in you [energizing and creating in you the power and desire], both to will and to work for His good pleasure and satisfaction and delight.

PHILIPPIANS 2:13 AMP

Portrait

In Christ, I am a freewoman, a daughter of God, and an heir of His promises (see Galatians 4:7).

DAY 1

Taking Stock

After starting your new lives in the Spirit, why are you now trying to become perfect by your own human effort? Have you experienced so much for nothing? Surely it was not in vain, was it? I ask you again, does God give you the Holy Spirit and work miracles among you because you obey the law? Of course not! It is because you believe the message you heard about Christ.
GALATIANS 3:3–5 NLT

Dear God, sometimes I get so caught up in what I think I should be doing that I completely forget to be. And then nothing seems right. There is dissonance within—and without. So help me to stop and take stock of my life and walk. I want to be who You want me to be—and leave the rest up to You.

DAY 2

Living the Life

"This is the promise that I will make to them after those days, says the Lord: 'I will put my teachings in their hearts and write them in their minds.'"
HEBREWS 10:16 GW

Lord, You have written Your words and imprinted Your ways upon my heart and mind. And the Spirit of Christ within me, that overwhelming instrument of Your love, compels me to want to do Your will. I love following Your voice, believing in Your promises, and living the life You have created me to live! May my children follow in my footsteps.

Day 3
Free in Deed!

Live freely, animated and motivated by God's Spirit. Then you won't feed the compulsions of selfishness. For there is a root of sinful self-interest in us that is at odds with a free spirit, just as the free spirit is incompatible with selfishness. These two ways of life are antithetical, so that you cannot live at times one way and at times another way according to how you feel on any given day. Why don't you choose to be led by the Spirit and so escape the erratic compulsions of a law-dominated existence?
GALATIANS 5:16–18 MSG

Whew, Lord. What angst I suffer when I'm trying to satisfy the law. I never seem to be able to get it right. When trying to please You with my head, everything I do seems empty. But when I live to please You with my heart, doing so out of my love for You, Your Spirit kicks in and it all comes together. Help me continue in the Spirit, Lord. Keep me free in deed!

Day 4
No Holds Barred

[Jesus] said, "I tell you the truth, unless you turn from your sins and become like little children, you will never get into the Kingdom of Heaven."
MATTHEW 18:3 NLT

I thank You for so many things, Lord, but especially for giving me children to have and to hold. They are a great reminder of how You want us to come to, trust, and love You—no holds barred. So I run to You now. Sweep me up in Your arms. Love me and mine. Keep us close to Your heart. Lead us to Your heaven.

DAY 5

The Driving Energy

*Love the Lord your God with all your heart and with all your soul
and with all your mind (intellect). This is the great (most important,
principal) and first commandment. And a second is like it:
You shall love your neighbor as [you do] yourself.*
MATTHEW 22:37–39 AMP

*Sometimes, Lord, I forget the basic rule—love. That's what it's all about. That's
the driving energy behind all that You do. Help me to keep in the forefront
of my mind that absolute love is to be the driving force behind all that I do
as well. Help me to love You, others, and myself just like You love me—
unconditionally and eternally.*

DAY 6

Unfathomable Love

*This is real love—not that we loved God, but that he loved
us and sent his Son as a sacrifice to take away our sins.*
1 JOHN 4:10 NLT

*I cannot imagine sacrificing my child for the sake of others. But You have
done that and more with the birth, life, and death of Your one and only Son,
Jesus. Words cannot express how grateful I am for that sacrifice and Your
unfathomable love. Help me to return the favor by being a conduit of Your
grace, love, and mercy for all people everywhere—beginning at home.*

DAY 7

Beginning and the End

"I am the Alpha and the Omega, the Beginning and the End.
To the thirsty I will give water without cost from the spring of the
water of life. Those who are victorious will inherit all this,
and I will be their God and they will be my children."
REVELATION 21:6–7 NIV

I love the idea that no matter how old I get, Lord, You will always be older.
You will always love me as Your little child. You have been here for me and
my children since the very beginning—and You will be with us all at the very
end. Thank You for setting us free to live and love You and each other. Thank
You for always being here.

CHAPTER 14
Growth

In the meadow, there were cotes and folds for sheep,
a house built for the nourishing and bringing up of those lambs,
the babes of those women that go on pilgrimage.
JOHN BUNYAN, *THE PILGRIM'S PROGRESS: PART 2*

• • • • • • •

*I*n this journey through life, we all begin our godly pilgrimage at different times and ages. Sometimes we are born into the church and so may be in Christ throughout our lives. At other times, we come into the faith after marriage or the birth of our own children. For some, the faith walk begins when we and our children are physically full grown. But no matter where or when we embark upon our journey, we are all working at becoming what we believe God has called us to be. And because we are still works in process, in the midst of our spiritual growth, not one of us is perfect.

Thus we can and should banish the grief, shame, self-doubt, and self-condemnation that come upon us when we make choices that have led us in the wrong direction, whether those choices had been made before—or after—the beginning of our faith walk. Because these missteps are merely part of our growth process, we should take care not to succumb to constant and consistent thoughts of our failings.

Nestled deep in God's grace, we can simply perceive any growing pains resulting from our missteps and imperfections as blessings, because for us who have not yet arrived, it's all about the journey. For our joy is found in the process of our growth! And finding that joy, amid our imperfection and immaturity, is what it's all about!

Second Peter 3:18 gives us some guidance about our development, for it says we are to "grow in grace (undeserved favor, spiritual strength) and recognition and knowledge and understanding of our Lord and Savior Jesus Christ (the Messiah)" (AMP). When we are first saved, we are infants in this new life in Christ. And as such, we are given milk because we cannot yet handle the meat of the Word (see 1 Corinthians 3:1–3). But thank the Lord, we need not remain mere babes.

As a mother, you would become alarmed and seek medical advice if your baby did not grow physically. So would God our Father be alarmed if we, His children, do not continue to grow spiritually. Yet many of us feel as if we can accomplish this growth in our own power. Perhaps we believe that if we try to do greater and greater things, we will reach the epitome of spirituality. Yet like the flowers and trees, we cannot *make* ourselves grow. That job has been left in the hands of our Father. We are mere plantings of the Lord—for His glory (see Isaiah 60:21; 61:3).

Can you just imagine an impatient child trying to increase his physical height? Yet do we not attempt to do something similar when we feel we have lost our passion for our faith? When we feel we have not gotten anywhere, that our lives have not improved one iota? Do we not stretch and strain to get back to the place from which we started? In this I-want-it-now culture, do we not feel discouraged if we aren't where we think we should be in our spiritual growth? So how do we remedy this situation?

What we need to do is stop trying to grow *into* grace but endeavor to grow *in* grace. Hannah Whitall Smith provides a wonderful analogy to help us understand this concept:

> *[Some Christians] are like a rosebush planted by a gardener in the hard, stony path with a view to its growing into the flower-bed, and which has of course dwindled and withered in consequence instead of flourishing and maturing.*

She likens such Christians to the Jews in the wilderness. All the fighting and wandering they did there did not help them obtain one inch of God's Promised

Land. To get possession of it, they needed to actually *enter* it. Once they did, they quickly began winning battles.

And we must do the same. In order to grow in grace, we have to plant ourselves in it, allowing our roots to go deep into this life hidden in Christ. Once we do, our spiritual growth will take off, and we will progress beyond our imagination.

Consider Rahab, an Old Testament harlot. She ran an inn in Jericho, the first threshold the no-longer-wandering Jews needed to cross to gain entrance into the Promised Land. Two spies, sent by Joshua to check out the city, stopped at her inn. There she not only professed her faith in their God (see Joshua 2:11) but risked her own life by hiding the spies and misleading their pursuers. Then she asked if the Israelites would spare her family when they attacked her city. The spies agreed to honor her request—but her family must be in her house, out of which she was to hang a red cord. She agreed and gave them safe directions out of town. Soon afterward, the Israelites marched around her city—for six days. During that time, Rahab did not panic but, knowing the God of Israel could and would be victorious, kept her faith—and God and His grace rewarded this woman and her family. But Rahab's story continued, as did the growth of her faith. In *Her Name Is Woman: Book 1*, Gien Karssen writes about Rahab:

> *Jericho only marked the beginning, for she had now found God. Her life began to blossom. There was no further longing for her former occupation; instead she became an honorable housewife. She, a heathen woman, lived among the Jewish people, married the Israelite Salmon, and had a child. If we were to evaluate her effectiveness as a mother by her sympathetic and wise son, Boaz, the husband of Ruth, then she did very well indeed, for Ruth becomes the great-grandmother of King David.*

And of course, Rahab, through her son Boaz, also became an ancestor of Jesus. Not only that, this former prostitute is one of two women, the princess Sarah being the other, listed in the hall of the famed faithful (see Hebrews 11:30–31). What an amazing growth she experienced in her God's grace!

So how do we believers in Christ accomplish such spiritual growth in God's unfathomable grace? First, we need to understand grace is not just God's unmerited favor, a gift He freely gives, requiring no action on our part. It is also His boundless, divine love poured out in multiple ways. Smith writes:

> *We seem to consider that divine love is hard and self-seeking and distant, concerned about its own glory, and indifferent to the fate of others. But if ever human love was tender and self-sacrificing and devoted, if ever it could bear and forbear, if ever it could suffer gladly for its loved one, if ever it was willing to pour itself out in a lavish abandonment for the comfort or pleasure of its objects, then infinitely more is divine love tender and self-sacrificing and devoted, and glad to bear and forbear, and suffer, and eager to lavish its best of gifts and blessings upon the objects of its love.*

Think of all the love of the best mothers, multiply it by infinity, and you may have scratched the surface of God's grace to us and love for us.

The second thing we need to do to grow in grace is to plant our souls in the very heart of God's love. We must steep ourselves in grace and allow it to surround us. We are to "consider the lilies of the field and learn thoroughly how they grow; they neither toil nor spin. Yet I tell you, even Solomon in all his magnificence (excellence, dignity, and grace) was not arrayed like one of these" (Matthew 6:28–29 AMP). It's all about allowing God to be in control and trusting Him to grow us as He desires. We are not to worry about the necessities of life, for doing so will not add one inch to our stature (see Matthew 6:27). In fact, worrying actually *impedes* our growth, for it reveals our doubts that God will, as promised, take care of us, just as He takes care of His lilies. It signals to God, and others, that since He may not truly take care of us, we must take things into our own hands. In doing so, we end up fighting or resisting God's promptings instead of yielding to Him and allowing Him to grow us up into the mothers He wants us to be.

This does not mean we are to remain idle in our spiritual growth. But it does mean we need to trust that this Maker of massive miracles, the One who grows children within our bodies, will give us and our kids the light, water, food, and clothes we need to live physically and everything we need spiritually. Growth will come as we wait upon Him and then peaceably and obediently do as He asks.

Third, to grow in grace you must understand that you have not chosen Christ but He has chosen you—just as He chose a prostitute to help His Israelites have victory in Jericho. He says that He has "[planted you], that you might go and bear fruit and keep on bearing" (John 15:16 AMP). That is how we got into His grace in the first place! He has planted us as He has the lily, which revels in God's sunshine, water, and soil. The lily neither stretches nor strains to get something it has already been given!

Fourth, acknowledge that you are planted in grace and then let God—the divine husbandman—have His way with you. Put yourself in the light of the Son of righteousness, allowing the dew from heaven to quench your thirst. And be pliable and yielding to what He would have you be!

If we expend effort trying to make ourselves grow spiritually, fussing and straining at every turn, our fruit will bear witness to our unnecessary toiling. We will be burned out—a common malady in church workers. We will wilt under stress. We will look for relief in all the wrong places instead of looking to God. Our eyes will be on our own selves or our self-dependence and self-effort.

Meanwhile, God is watching our futile efforts, shaking His head as we run around like chickens with our heads cut off. Moms, why do we feel we must do it all on our own? Did we create the baby that grows within our womb? Did we, through some effort on our part, form its tiny fingernails, its crop of hair, its heart, lungs, and eyes? No! God did it all. The only effort we expended was to take care of our bodies while the baby grew within us. Then in God's timing (and with a bit of pushing on our part), the baby came forth and into our arms.

As God makes the baby grow without it even being aware that it is indeed growing, He has planted us to grow spiritually. And we are utterly helpless to do anything but allow Him to do so and not hinder His work within us. For when we hinder Him, we expend all our energy, grow exhausted, and suddenly find ourselves growing backward rather than forward. We would be wise to tap into the lily's secret and grow in God's way.

Of course, we are not actually lilies. We are human beings with a modicum of intelligence, a certain degree of power, and personal responsibility. Yet that's just where our hindrance to God's work comes in. Smith writes:

> *What the lily is by nature we must be by an intelligent and free surrender. To be one of the lilies means an interior abandonment of the rarest kind. It means that we are to be infinitely passive, and yet infinitely active also: passive as regards self and its workings, active as regards attention and response to God.*

Would that we would be like the reformed Rahab—passive as far as waiting for God's people to rescue her but active as far as putting down the scarlet cord.

So, ladies, know that whether or not you are conscious of it, God has made you to grow. If you find yourself straining once again to be your own gardener, seeding when you think it's needed, and perhaps even pruning yourself, stop! Then step aside and allow God to work while being attentive and responsive to Him and His Word. When you do, you will be blessed and become more intimate in your knowledge of God. Each one of you will prosper, bringing forth fruit, "some an hundredfold, some sixtyfold, some thirtyfold" (Matthew 13:8 KJV).

> *"The tree grew huge and strong. Its top reached the sky and it could be seen from the four corners of the earth. Its leaves were beautiful, its fruit abundant—enough food for everyone! Wild animals found shelter under it, birds nested in its branches, everything living was fed and sheltered by it."*
> DANIEL 4:11–12 MSG

PATH MARKERS

Promise

Blessed is the person who. . .delights in the teachings of the LORD and reflects on his teachings day and night. He is like a tree planted beside streams—a tree that produces fruit in season and whose leaves do not wither. He succeeds in everything he does.

PSALM 1:1–3 GW

Proof

"For through the law I died to the law so that I might live for God. I have been crucified with Christ and I no longer live, but Christ lives in me. The life I now live in the body, I live by faith in the Son of God, who loved me and gave himself for me. I do not set aside the grace of God, for if righteousness could be gained through the law, Christ died for nothing!"

GALATIANS 2:19–21 NIV

Provision

"Here's what I want you to do: Find a quiet, secluded place so you won't be tempted to role-play before God. Just be there as simply and honestly as you can manage. The focus will shift from you to God, and you will begin to sense his grace."

MATTHEW 6:6 MSG

Portrait

In Christ, I am growing in the grace and knowledge of the Lord (see 2 Peter 3:18).

Mind-Renewing Prayers

Day 1
What Joy!

Blessed (happy, enviably fortunate, and spiritually prosperous—possessing the happiness produced by the experience of God's favor and especially conditioned by the revelation of His grace, regardless of their outward conditions) are the pure in heart, for they shall see God!
MATTHEW 5:8 AMP

I am happy in the fact, Lord, that each day I am getting to know You better and better. I believe in Your promises. I revel in Your fathomless grace. Regardless of what is going on around me, I know that I and the ones I love are safe in, loved by, and favored by You. What joy have I!

Day 2
Grace and Glory

For the LORD God is our sun and our shield. He gives us grace and glory. The LORD will withhold no good thing from those who do what is right.
PSALM 84:11 NLT

Each and every day, Lord, I have decisions to make. Give me the wisdom to make the right ones. Shed Your light upon my path; shield me with Your presence. Bless me with Your grace and glory. Help me not to just do the next thing—but to do the next right thing. Show me Your goodness as I endeavor to walk this pathway with You.

Day 3

The Boldness

*But the apostles stayed there a long time, preaching boldly about the
grace of the Lord. And the Lord proved their message was true by
giving them power to do miraculous signs and wonders.*

ACTS 14:3 NLT

*I am astounded at all the gifts You have showered upon me—and all the gifts
still in Your hands! Your grace, Your unconditional love, Your faith in who I
am, Your patience that I am still a work in progress is overwhelming. Help me
to continue to have faith and rest in You. Give me the boldness to leave all—
myself, my kids, our dreams, our desires—in Your hands.*

Day 4

Amazing Grace

*"We believe that we are all saved the same way,
by the undeserved grace of the Lord Jesus."*

ACTS 15:11 NLT

*That You would save a wretch like me, God, is amazing. I didn't start out my
life knowing You well. But after seeing the miracle of children entering the
world, I knew there was another way—and it was through You. Thank You
for saving me and for Your amazing grace. May Your light within me attract
others to You.*

DAY 5
Leftover Energy

And God is able to make all grace abound toward you,
that you, always having all sufficiency in all things,
may have an abundance for every good work.
2 CORINTHIANS 9:8 NKJV

I'm done trying to do things all in my own power—because in those instances
I find myself coming from my mind, not my heart. But in Your kingdom,
God, heart is what it's all about. So I'm here once again, asking You to pour
Your good grace upon me so I can do all things through You—and have some
energy left over for my children.

DAY 6
Taking a Backseat

And He [Jesus] said to me, "My grace is sufficient for you,
for My strength is made perfect in weakness." Therefore most gladly
I will rather boast in my infirmities, that the power of Christ may rest upon me.
2 CORINTHIANS 12:9 NKJV

It's weird but true, Lord. When I'm weak, You are working Your best stuff
through me. So please help me (and my ego) take a backseat. Then go ahead
and pour Your power upon me. Help me to find my strength in You every day
and in every way, as I continually leave the driving to You.

Day 7
Solid God

*He who leans on, trusts in, and is confident in his riches shall fall,
but the [uncompromisingly] righteous shall flourish like a green bough.*
PROVERBS 11:28 AMP

*Money is so fleeting, Lord. Sometimes it just seems to slip through my fingers.
But You are solid. You are what I have faith in. Your love and light working
within me not only grow me up in Your grace but grow my children up
as well. Help us, Lord, to keep our eyes on You and our ears open to Your
command!*

CHAPTER 15
Service

Then said Christiana, Though the highways have been unoccupied heretofore, and though the travelers have been made in time past to walk through by-paths, it must not be so now I am risen. Now "I am risen a mother in Israel" (Judges 5:6, 7).

JOHN BUNYAN, *THE PILGRIM'S PROGRESS: PART 2*

• • • • • • •

*W*hen first embarking upon the journey in this life of Christ, many are full of joy and enthusiasm, wanting to do some sort of service for our wonderful Lord because we have learned Jesus' command to be the "servant of all" (Mark 9:35 KJV)—*in*side and *out*side of our church. But as time passes, we may begin to feel like what was once our joy in serving has become a chore. When that happens, we have moved from the freedom we experienced as Christ's workers, with the "May I?" of love on our lips, to the frenzied activity of anxious slaves, with the "Must I?" of duty expressed through gritted teeth.

And here we are not just talking about working for the church. It's *all* the work that we do for one and all—for because we are Christians, all work *is* Christian work! Thus, this includes not only teaching Sunday school or serving on the church board but also raising godly children, obeying our godly husband, helping our parents when needed, keeping our relationship with God intact, and being an example to those not yet saved.

When we feel fretful, stressed, disdainful, worn out, and tied up in knots about *any* of our work, or when we have an impending desire to find our way *out* of serving others, we can be sure we have stepped off our pathway and embarked upon a route of bondage. At that point, we must immediately step back and look at our situation with the goal of breaking through to receive the power that awaits mothers hidden in Christ.

The following are six bondages and breakthroughs to freedom that we moms may encounter and employ, respectively.

The first bondage is *flagging energy and will to do God's work*. Feeling as if we are no longer strong enough to accomplish what God has asked us to do, we do it either begrudgingly or not at all. Yet the fact is that God has intended us to do what He wills, for He has written it upon our hearts and planted the seeds within our minds as part of His new covenant with us (see Hebrews 8:10). He is working within you and through you to make your work not a duty but a pleasure and is giving you the energy to do it (see Philippians 2:13).

Whatever strength you may have to do God's will is actually your biggest weakness (see Romans 6:13 KJV) because it can hinder what God wants to do *through* you (see 2 Corinthians 12:9). Look at it this way: You've probably played patty-cake with your infant who at that age lacks hand-eye coordination and muscular strength, so you lift up your baby's arms, clap his hands together, then pat them, roll them, and open up his arms for the grand finale. Your baby does nothing but yield himself up to *your* control. That is *his* part; the controlling, the responsibility, is *your* part. The child has neither skill nor capacity to do the motions to patty-cake. His utter weakness is his greatest strength, and it provides his greatest delight!

To break through this bondage of flagging energy and desire to do God's work, pray. Ask God to help you to understand He has given you the power and longing to do what He has called you to do. Envision Him filling you up with His Abba-Daddy strength and desire. Working in God's power will give you the energy to change that umpteenth diaper!

The second form of bondage is *thinking you are not good enough to be serving in a particular way*. You can't believe God has called you to join the worship team, serve on the church board, or chair vacation Bible school. The way to break through is to understand God has already gone before you and prepared the way for you (see John 10:3–4). Build up your God-confidence by nurturing your spirit in the Word. Hunger for His promises, His truths, and apply them to your heart (see 2 Timothy 3:15). Reading God's Word daily, slowly, and prayerfully will feed your minds and spirits, building you into the mother He wants you to be.

The third bondage of service is *doing things to exalt yourself or with the expectation of receiving an external reward*. Being so anxious to do something well and right to impress people will not only put pressure on you but fill you with worry. And if you're struggling to exalt yourself, you're taking the glory from Christ.

The remedy? Get your eyes off yourself and back on God, working for Him— and no other (see Colossians 3:23–24). Be a God gratifier—not a people pleaser. Forget self. Humility will empower you to go forward, knowing that everything you do is for the Lord—and no one else! Taking heed that it's all about God will help you leave your comfort zone and do what He's called you to do well!

The fourth form of bondage is *experiencing discouragement and despair*. The outreach project that was your idea hasn't brought anyone new into the church. You are ready to step down from being on the committee, to throw in the towel. This attitude indicates a lack of trust in God.

The remedy for discouragement is rolling every care off on the Lord (see Psalm 37:5 AMP). Instead of giving up, lean harder on God. He will see you through! It's the evil one pointing out all your faults and feeding your misgivings. Pray and trust God to give you persistence as well as the courage and care you need.

To break through despair, cultivate joy within yourself. Recognize God has an awesome plan for your life (see Jeremiah 29:11). Take joy in that promise! Thank God for all He has done in your life already—and what He plans to do in your future. When you do, you will be so renewed that you won't be able to stop praising God for the blessings awaiting you!

The fifth form of bondage is *feeling you are doing too little or not enough*. The remedy is understanding your responsibility in the matter. You are accountable for doing what God has called you to do and what He has given you the talents to perform—nothing more and nothing less. Smith writes:

No one individual is responsible for all the work in the world, but only for a small share. Our duty ceases to be universal, and becomes personal and individual. The master does not say, "Go and do everything," but He marks out an especial path for each one of us, and gives to each one of us an especial duty.

Remember that the work is God's, that He gives to each "according to his [or her] ability" (Matthew 25:15 TNIV). What a relief that you are just His instrument! Rest in knowing the Lord will tell you how and what you should be doing (see Jeremiah 42:3 NASB), and you need not entertain what-ifs. So take on your responsibilities in God's strength, under His constant guidance, and by His leading. Just fill one sphere of responsibility, for one door opens to larger things, and another to still larger, until you find yourself doing, in God's power, tasks you never believed or imagined possible (see Matthew 25:21). And by working in accordance with His timing, you'll be *exactly* where He wants you to be.

The sixth form of bondage is *reflections after completing any endeavor*. Afterthoughts of this type come in two varieties. Either we congratulate ourselves upon the endeavor's success and are lifted up, or we are distressed over its failure and are utterly cast down. The breakthrough is to put the final results of any task in God's hands—and *leave them there* (see Philippians 3:13)! Know that God, like any good parent, is always pleased with your efforts and move on to the next thing. Refuse to worry. Simply ask God to override any mistakes and to bless your efforts as He chooses.

Take a look at the Old Testament prophet, homemaker, wife, and judge named Deborah (Judges 4–5). Her motivating power was God and His will for herself and her people. Plugged into Him and His Word, she was more than spiritually fit, nourished, wise, and unworried. She continually sought God's guidance—then heeded it, leading His panic-stricken children to victory. Because of her amazing passion for doing the will of God; her unflagging energy, courage, and persistence; her positive attitude in the face of impossible odds; her commitment to living to give God all the glory; her reliance upon the Lord of Lords; her determination to do God's work; and her joyful after-victory songwriting, she was named the "mother for Israel" (Judges 5:7 NLT). Wow! The mother of a nation! After her, fifty years of peace followed. Oh, what a woman!

Through all your serving, follow Deborah's model. When you do, may the results lead God to say:

"Well done, good and faithful servant; you were faithful over a few things, I will make you ruler over many things. Enter into the joy of your lord."
MATTHEW 25:21 NKJV

Path Markers

Promise

"For I know the plans that I have for you," declares the Lord, "plans for welfare and not for calamity to give you a future and a hope."

JEREMIAH 29:11 NASB

Proof

There was a believer in Joppa named Tabitha (which in Greek is Dorcas). She was always doing kind things for others and helping the poor. About this time she became ill and died. Her body was washed for burial and laid in an upstairs room. But the believers had heard that Peter was nearby at Lydda, so they sent two men to beg him, "Please come as soon as possible!"

So Peter returned with them; and as soon as he arrived, they took him to the upstairs room. The room was filled with widows who were weeping and showing him the coats and other clothes Dorcas had made for them. But Peter asked them all to leave the room; then he knelt and prayed. Turning to the body he said, "Get up, Tabitha." And she opened her eyes! When she saw Peter, she sat up! He gave her his hand and helped her up. Then he called in the widows and all the believers, and he presented her to them alive.

ACTS 9:36–41 NLT

Provision

[Not in your own strength] for it is God Who is all the while effectually at work in you [energizing and creating in you the power and desire], both to will and to work for His good pleasure and satisfaction and delight.

PHILIPPIANS 2:13 AMP

Portrait

In Christ, I am strong enough to do whatever God calls me to do (see Philippians 4:13).

MIND-RENEWING PRAYERS

DAY 1

My Energizer

[The Lord] told me, My grace is enough; it's all you need. My strength comes into its own in your weakness. Once I heard that, I was glad to let it happen. I quit focusing on the handicap and began appreciating the gift. It was a case of Christ's strength moving in on my weakness. Now I take limitations in stride, and with good cheer, these limitations that cut me down to size—abuse, accidents, opposition, bad breaks. I just let Christ take over! And so the weaker I get, the stronger I become.

2 CORINTHIANS 12:9 MSG

Lord, You are my energizer, my motivating power. With You on my side, working through me, amazing things happen! Things beyond my wildest imagination. And it's all because I'm doing it in Your strength. I'm letting You take me over. No matter what happens, I have joy. That's taking all the pressure off and allowing me to become the mother You envisioned me to be!

Day 2
Best in Mind

Every day [with its new reasons] will I bless You [affectionately and gratefully praise You]; yes, I will praise Your name forever and ever.
Psalm 145:2 AMP

Lord, I'm living in the moment, finding joy in each little area I serve. Whether I am the cook, chief bottle washer, curfew sheriff, nursery monitor, or simply being "Mom," I am looking for, and expecting to find, things for which to praise You, each and every day. What will it be today, Lord? What do You have in mind for me and mine?

Day 3
All the Reward I Need

When you give to the poor, don't let anyone know about it. Then your gift will be given in secret. Your Father knows what is done in secret, and he will reward you.
Matthew 6:3–4 CEV

I love it, Jesus! It seems as if the more I give, the more I get in return—although at a much better exchange rate! When I give of my time and money to those less fortunate, I reap so much more—the joy of serving in secret—because effort is just between You and me. Becoming more like You is all the reward I need.

DAY 4

Loving It!

Do what the LORD wants, and he will give you your heart's desire.
Let the LORD lead you and trust him to help.
PSALM 37:4–5 CEV

I really went out on a limb, Lord. I stretched myself, my faith, and my family to go where You were leading, trusting You in more ways than one. And amazingly enough, my efforts have borne such wonderful fruit! Now that I have met this challenge, I find I'm really loving it! So I'm ready for the next step! Lead on, Lord, whenever You're ready. I'll follow You anywhere.

DAY 5

Goal Lover's Travels

I'm not saying that I have this all together, that I have it made. But I am well on my way, reaching out for Christ, who has so wondrously reached out for me. Friends, don't get me wrong: By no means do I count myself an expert in all of this, but I've got my eye on the goal, where God is beckoning us onward—to Jesus. I'm off and running, and I'm not turning back.
PHILIPPIANS 3:12–14 MSG

You, Lord, are an amazing goal setter. I am standing where I never before envisioned myself to be. And it's all because of You. You have increased my faith a hundredfold. There's no going back now. It's You and me, Lord— and all to Your glory, Your love, Your strength, Your courage. We're in together— deep. This fathomless faith I've obtained— it's so cool.

Day 6
Such a Time

*"Who knows whether you have come
to the kingdom for such a time as this?"*
ESTHER 4:14 NKJV

I'm uncertain, God, as to where You want me to be, what You want me to do,
when You want me to do it. But I know You are calling me. So please, Lord,
make it clear. Show me the step You want me to take. Make me the mother of
man and daughter of God You've created me to be. What shall I do in Your
kingdom, for such a time as this?

Day 7
My Forever Joy

*Well done, you upright (honorable, admirable) and faithful servant!
You have been faithful and trustworthy over a little; I will put
you in charge of much. Enter into and share the joy
(the delight, the blessedness) which your master enjoys.*
MATTHEW 25:21 AMP

Lord, I long for Your praise! I want to do Your will. Give me a chance. What do
You want me to do? Where? When? How? What gifts do You see in me? All these
questions are leading me, I believe, to where You want me to be—which right
now is just where I am. That knowledge allows me to be patient, to relax in the
present, waiting upon You, in Your presence.

Chapter 16

The Daily Walk and Talk

Now they had not gone far, but a great mist and darkness fell
upon them all, so that they could scarce, for a great while,
see the one the other; wherefore they were forced, for some time,
to feel for one another by words; for they walked not by sight.
John Bunyan, *The Pilgrim's Progress: Part 2*

• • • • • • • •

We are women. And that generally means we are great talkers. Some of us may even be great *walkers*. The question is, does our daily life—our walk *and* our talk—reflect the higher life, the life hidden in Christ? Do people see us as a "peculiar people" (1 Peter 2:9 KJV)—not conformed to this world but transformed by the renewing of our minds (see Romans 12:2)? Or are we so satisfied with our lives that, in almost every aspect, there seems to be no discernible difference between us and non-Christians?

Let's face it. There are many believers who are discouraged, depressed, anxious, gloomy, negative, frowning, self-indulgent, and armed with sharp tongues or bitter spirits. And although they may be respected Christian leaders or avid workers in the church, they seem to know nothing about the realities of the higher life in Christ. Or they may have discovered the blessings of walking as Christ walked but they only assume that mantle when with their minister or other Christians. When they get home, where the rubber truly meets the road, they become other persons entirely, losing their tempers with their children, succumbing to the temptations of the world, bragging about their accomplishments, manipulating others to gain what they want, and so forth.

Although you may not be a professional preacher, your life, your words, and your behavior do demonstrate your beliefs to others—especially to your children. If you call yourself a Christian, when others see you they should see Christ, for "clearly you are an epistle of Christ" (2 Corinthians 3:3 NKJV). Hannah Whitall Smith writes, "The life hid with Christ in God is a hidden life, as to its source, but it must not be hidden as to its practical results."

If we are to be Christian mothers who walk the walk and talk the talk, we had best be hidden in Christ 24–7, not just in front of other believers and the minister, but at home, at work, everywhere we go, and in everything we do!

A good example of such a woman who walked the walk and talked the talk of a joy-filled life in spite of circumstances is the New Testament's Elizabeth. Although she and her husband, Zachariah (both from the priestly line of Aaron), were elderly and childless, they "were righteous in the sight of God, *walking* blamelessly in all the commandments and requirements of the Lord" (Luke 1:6 AMP, emphasis added). Did you notice the word *walking* there?

This old couple was following God heart, mind, body, and soul. But even then, He had not chosen to bless them with a child. Yet apparently they were not displaying anger, discouragement, or bitterness against God, for no one could say anything against their behavior.

Then, by some miracle, their prayer was answered! While Zachariah was serving in God's temple, the angel Gabriel told him, "Your prayer has been heard. Elizabeth, your wife, will bear a son by you. You are to name him John. You're going to leap like a gazelle for joy, and not only you—many will delight in his birth. He'll achieve great stature with God" (Luke 1:13–15 MSG). (Notice the words *joy* and *delight* in this message from God.)

So apparently Elizabeth and Zachariah had persisted in their prayer for a child. And it was finally being answered. About this, Matthew Henry writes, "Prayers of faith are *filed* in heaven, and are not *forgotten*, though the thing prayed for is not presently *given* in."

Gabriel continued his announcement to Zachariah:

"He [John] will be filled with the Holy Spirit while yet in his mother's

womb. And he will turn many of the sons of Israel back to the Lord their God. It is he who will go as a forerunner before Him in the spirit and power of Elijah, to turn the hearts of the fathers back to the children, and the disobedient to the attitude of the righteous, so as to make ready a people prepared for the Lord." (Luke 1:15–17 NASB)

Yet because Zachariah chose not to believe but to request a sign from God, the angel told him, "Because you won't believe me, you'll be unable to say a word until the day of your son's birth. Every word I've spoken to you will come true on time—*God's* time" (Luke 1:19–20 MSG, emphasis in original).

Through signs to his wife, Zachariah probably made it clear to her what had happened at the temple. So even though she did not hear the angel's words directly, Elizabeth must've believed, continued, as always, to walk by faith—not sight—and in time, conceived. "She kept herself in seclusion for five months, saying, 'This is the way the Lord has dealt with me in the days when He looked with favor upon me, to take away my disgrace among men' " (Luke 1:24–25 NASB).

While Elizabeth was in seclusion, her younger cousin Mary was also visited by Gabriel. In fact, *he's* the one who told Mary that the barren Elizabeth was "six months pregnant! Nothing, you see, is impossible with God" (Luke 1:36–37 MSG). This amazing information must've boosted Mary's faith tremendously!

So here we have two women faithfully and dutifully following God, recognizing the extent of His amazing power, and fully allowing His Spirit to use them for His glory. They had been walking the walk by faith, not yet sight, and now Mary ran off to talk to her cousin about their blessings! Of this, Matthew Henry writes, "It is very beneficial and comfortable for those that have a good work of grace begun in their souls, to consult those who are in the same case. They will find that, as in water face answer to face, so doth the heart of man to man, of Christian to Christian," and may we say, of mother to mother.

Upon their meeting, Elizabeth continued to bear the fruit of God's Spirit.

When Mary greeted her, the baby in Elizabeth's womb leaped for joy. Filled with the Holy Spirit, Elizabeth sang her humble, nonenvious, and joyful song:

> *"Blessed are you among women, and blessed is the child you will bear! But why am I so favored, that the mother of my Lord should come to me? As soon as the sound of your greeting reached my ears, the baby in my womb leaped for joy. Blessed is she who has believed that the Lord would fulfill his promises to her!" (Luke 1:42–45 NIV)*

John Bunyan, in *The Pilgrim's Progress: Part 2*, writes, "When the Saviour was come, women rejoiced in him before either man or angel." What a milestone for women! What a privilege for our sex! And Elizabeth—what a model for all mothers—and mothers-to-be! As a humble and gracious conduit of God's Spirit, she truly exemplifies how to walk the walk and talk the talk.

So how do we, modern Christian moms, follow in the footsteps of Elizabeth? We begin at the beginning.

Early in the morning, setting our minds on heavenly things, not things of this earth (see Colossians 3:2), we are to "seek first the kingdom of God and His righteousness" (Matthew 6:33 NKJV). Before our feet hit the floor, we can determine to clothe ourselves in Christ and practice the presence of God.

Acknowledge that God is present here and now. Ask, then allow Him to fill you to the brim with His joy and knowledge, His power and strength. Know and believe He is with you—in each and every aspect of your life and day!

With Christ's mantle without, the Spirit's power within, and God's presence surrounding each of us here and now, we will be expressing our Lord and Savior to everyone we meet! We will find ourselves walking as Christ walked. We will be a peculiar people—empowered, loving, keeping no record of wrongs, returning good for evil, gentle, meek, kind, and yielding. We will not stand up for our own rights but will stand up for those of others, doing nothing for our glory but all for the glory of God. And we will be Christlike in private as well as in public, every hour of every day and not just on special occasions. We will not be plagued with anxieties or what-ifs because we know that *only today* is ours, given to us by our loving God. He has taken back all our yesterdays, and all our tomorrows are still in His hands. We will live happily in the consciousness of here and now. We will meet challenges bravely and persistently rise above obstacles without discouragement.

David Hume has said, "He is happy whose circumstances suit his temper; but he is more excellent who can suit his temper to any circumstance." How true! Here we must reflect, asking ourselves if our good tempers remain, no matter what. Are we still living close to God when the washer breaks, we lose a job, a prayer goes unanswered, the car stalls, the computer dies, or a child throws a tantrum?

Perhaps some of you are not there yet, but after reading about this higher life, you have begun to hear God's voice whispering, "This is the way, walk in it" (Isaiah 30:21 NKJV). Perhaps you have begun to feel uneasy about certain aspects of your life, attitudes, or habits. Perhaps you have not been happy about some of the words that have been coming out of your mouth.

While walking the walk, we would be wise to be sure our words are of encouragement or instruction only—or to say no words at all. My mother would often tell me, "If you don't have anything nice to say, don't say anything at all." If we all followed that adage, chances are we would be mothers of few words. Proverbs 17:28 tells us that "even fools are thought wise if they keep silent, and discerning if they hold their tongues" (TNIV). Would that we would seek out the conversation of moms who have believing souls, moms who are on the same path as we are, for there we can boost each other's joy and sometimes soothe each other's heartaches. We can praise God together, pray together, love together. We can lift each other, encourage each other, and, when needed, admonish each other.

Let's stop twittering endless hours away, blogging about inanities, and telling people how we're spending our days instead of actually living them. Let's exchange the compulsion to satisfy our obsession for material things with the hunger and thirst for God's Word. Let's open up our Bible and worship the one true God instead of turning to *American Idol* for entertainment.

As mothers, we *can* change this world—one person, one soul, one spirit at a time, beginning with ourselves. Seeking truth, striving to serve others, and doing God's will are more important now than ever before. The only solution to the emptiness of our lives and the fruitlessness of living in a society that seeks only to have more is a transparent Christianity where others look at us and see Christ alone.

Are you tired of trying to live up to the world's expectations? Are you ready for a radical spiritual transformation? You can do it! "With God all things are possible" (Matthew 19:26 TNIV), and blessed is she who believes it (Luke 1:45)! Put everything you are and hope to be in the hands of the Father of lights, who has promised us "every good and perfect gift" (see James 1:17). And cultivate joy.

Move forward in the power of quietness, knowing God surrounds you, Christ is within you, and the Holy Spirit guides you. Recognize that your energies should not be used exclusively to pursue worldly means but to seek first His kingdom, knowing He will provide whatever you need. As you begin to live this God-empowered life, living and loving in Christ will become a holy habit.

Envision yourself enfolded in God's love and power, just as you once enfolded your little child in your arms. Know that, in God, nothing can harm you, so rest in His care. Leave with Him yesterday. He is guiding you today. He is crowding tomorrow full of blessings and opportunities—so you have only cause for peace and expectancy. Rejoice in His safety, for you are His precious child. Know that there is nothing to fear, for behind you is God's infinite power. In front of you are endless possibilities, and you are surrounded by opportunity.

How wonderful to be abandoned to the guidance of our divine Master and fearlessly living our lives to His glory. The best part is that we need not do anything in our own power. He will provide all the strength and courage we need. Our part is merely to yield ourselves to Him, and His part is to work. He will never give us a command for which He has not equipped us with the power and strength to obey. He will never leave us nor forsake us but eternally lead the way.

"The LORD is the one who goes ahead of you;
He will be with you. . . . Do not fear or be dismayed."
DEUTERONOMY 31:8 NASB

$\mathscr{P}$ATH MARKERS

$\mathscr{P}$romise

Don't love the world's ways. Don't love the world's goods. Love of the world squeezes out love for the Father. Practically everything that goes on in the world—wanting your own way, wanting everything for yourself, wanting to appear important—has nothing to do with the Father. It just isolates you from him. The world and all its wanting, wanting, wanting is on the way out—but whoever does what God wants is set for eternity.

1 JOHN 2:15–17 MSG

$\mathscr{P}$roof

But we have this treasure in jars of clay to show that this all-surpassing power is from God and not from us. We are hard pressed on every side, but not crushed; perplexed, but not in despair; persecuted, but not abandoned; struck down, but not destroyed. We always carry around in our body the death of Jesus, so that the life of Jesus may also be revealed in our body. . . . Therefore we do not lose heart. Though outwardly we are wasting away, yet inwardly we are being renewed day by day. For our light and momentary troubles are achieving for us an eternal glory that far outweighs them all. So we fix our eyes not on what is seen, but on what is unseen, since what is seen is temporary, but what is unseen is eternal.

2 CORINTHIANS 4:7–10, 16–18 NIV

$\mathscr{P}$rovision

For we are God's handiwork, created in Christ Jesus to do good works, which God prepared in advance for us to do.

EPHESIANS 2:10 TNIV

Portrait

In Christ, I am spiritually transformed with energy, strength, and purpose every day (see Romans 12:1–2).

Mind-Renewing Prayers

Day 1

Finding Joy

We are always confident, knowing that while we are at home in the body we are absent from the Lord. For we walk by faith, not by sight.

2 Corinthians 5:6–7 NKJV

Jesus, I want to be like Elizabeth, finding joy in each and every situation, believing You will be true to Your Word, sinking my teeth into Your promises. Regardless of what my circumstances seem to be on this earthly plane, I know that You are working out a plan for my life. So my eyes are on You—and nowhere else!

Day 2

Through the Mists

We have the mind of Christ (the Messiah) and do
hold the thoughts (feelings and purposes) of His heart.
1 CORINTHIANS 2:16 AMP

Bring me good news from Your Word every morning, Lord. Nourish me with
Your songs of hope and deliverance. I expect good things from You, Lord,
and am looking for Your light, Your beacon of love, through the mists that
sometimes surround me. Feed the flame You have hidden in my heart. Make
my mind, body, and soul Yours.

Day 3

The True Path

If we say we are his, we must follow the example of Christ.
1 JOHN 2:6 CEV

I am looking only to You, Christ. For You are the true path. Lead me to fellow
pilgrims who are walking this earth with children in tow, moms who I can
encourage and who will encourage me. I want to share Your joy and Your
peace with others. I want to be a true believer and liver of Your Word. Show me
the way. Lead me on. My life is in Your hands.

Day 4
A Conduit of Your Love

Your old life is dead. Your new life, which is your real life—
even though invisible to spectators—is with Christ in God. He is your life.
When Christ (your real life, remember) shows up again on this earth,
you'll show up, too—the real you, the glorious you.
Meanwhile, be content with obscurity, like Christ.
COLOSSIANS 3:3–4 MSG

Work through me, Jesus. Use me as Your vessel. Help me to just be a conduit of Your love and power. May I, like John the Baptist, become lesser so that You can be seen more vividly. For You are what and who life is all about. You are the true Spirit, Life, and Light. And in You only do I live, move, and have my being, every day and in every way.

Day 5
Just a Pilgrim

Set your minds and keep them set on what is above (the higher things),
not on the things that are on the earth.
COLOSSIANS 3:2 AMP

I am just a pilgrim on this earth, Lord. I am a stranger and a foreigner here. But You have given me an opportunity to spread Your light amid this darkness. Fill my mind with the treasures of Your heaven. Help me to shine Your light and hope upon my children. And may I give You all the praise for Your wonder, majesty, and promises as I trust in You each day.

Day 6
Finding Forgiveness

Be gentle and forbearing with one another and, if one has a difference
(a grievance or complaint) against another, readily pardoning each other;
even as the Lord has [freely] forgiven you, so must you also [forgive].
COLOSSIANS 3:13 AMP

If I am to walk as You walked, Lord, I need to find forgiveness—no matter
who has done what. And sometimes that is difficult. But I'm sure there are
times You find it hard to forgive me. So I am calling on Your strength,
Your peace, Your power to forgive another. At the same time, I thank You for
forgiving me.

Day 7
My Now

Exercise daily in God—no spiritual flabbiness, please!
Workouts in the gymnasium are useful, but a disciplined life in God is far
more so, making you fit both today and forever. You can count on this.
Take it to heart. This is why we've thrown ourselves
into this venture so totally. We're banking on the living God,
Savior of all men and women, especially believers.
1 TIMOTHY 4:7–8 MSG

I'm making it a daily habit, Lord, to hand my life, my past, and my future
over to You. Help me to remember to live my life one moment at a time, for
that is all I really have. I cannot change the past. I cannot do anything about
the future today. So I am giving You my all; I am giving You me—each and
every moment. You are my now.

CHAPTER 17
The Joy of Obedience

[The Interpreter or Holy Spirit said to Mercy,] Thy setting out is good;
for thou hast given credit to the truth. Thou art a Ruth; who did, for the love
that she bore to Naomi, and to the Lord her God, leave father and mother,
and the land of her nativity, to come out, and go with a people that she knew
not heretofore. "The Lord recompense thy work; and a full reward be given
thee of the Lord God of Israel, under whose wings thou art come to truth."
JOHN BUNYAN, *THE PILGRIM'S PROGRESS: PART 2*

• • • • • • •

*J*f you have been fortunate in this life, you have at one time or another had
someone you really and truly loved. Because of that love, you found yourself
desiring to do anything and everything for him or her. No sacrifice was too big for
this especially loved one. When you were separated from this person, you longed for
him or her to return to you quickly, if possible.

As mothers, we often have such a special relationship with our children,
particularly when they are infants. Although at times we may feel we need a break
from changing diapers, getting up for 4:00 a.m. feedings, and fighting raging
fevers, when we do get time away, our tiny, precious one consumes our every
thought. We almost can't wait until we hold our child in our arms again.

Whether or not this special person in your life is your child, friend, sister,
brother, or lover, it's almost as if two separate persons—you and the other—had
become one in thought, word, and deed. Smith describes such a bond like this:

> *A union of soul takes place, which makes all that belongs to one the*
> *property of the other. Separate interests and separate paths in life are*

no longer possible. . . . Love gives all, and must have all in return. The wishes of one become binding obligations to the other, and the deepest desire of each heart is that it may know every secret wish or longing of the other in order that it may fly on the wings of the wind to gratify it.

The Old Testament woman Ruth had such a relationship with her mother-in-law, Naomi. Sounds almost impossible, doesn't it? But it's true! Naomi, her husband, and their two sons had come to Moab because of a drought in their homeland of Israel. Within the ten-year span she spent in Moab, Naomi's husband died, her sons each took a wife, and then her sons died—childless! So upon hearing the famine in Judah was over, Naomi decided to head back home. In spite of her insistence that her daughters-in-law Orpah and Ruth remain behind and go back to their mothers' houses, Ruth would not. Instead, she told Naomi:

Intreat me not to leave thee, or to return from following after thee: for whither thou goest, I will go; and where thou lodgest, I will lodge: thy people shall be my people, and thy God my God: where thou diest, will I die, and there will I be buried: the LORD do so to me, and more also, if ought but death part thee and me. (Ruth 1:16–17 KJV)

Wow! Ruth neither complained about her lot in life nor talked about how much she was giving up to stick with her mother-in-law. Instead, with quiet determination and dedication, she, along with her mother-in-law, began the arduous 120-mile trek to a land she had never set foot in before, without much money or a protector. Upon their arrival in Bethlehem, Ruth began working in the fields of Boaz (Naomi's husband's relative), gleaning grain, and bringing back her small harvest to joyfully place it in Naomi's hands.

Boaz, struck by the faithfulness of Ruth, said to her, "The LORD recompense thy work, and a full reward be given thee of the LORD God of Israel, under whose wings thou art come to trust" (Ruth 2:12 KJV). Later Naomi suggested Ruth make an overture of fidelity to Boaz. In response, the ever-obedient Ruth said, "All that thou sayest unto me I will do" (Ruth 3:5 KJV). (Would that our children be as obedient to us as Ruth to Naomi!) As a result of her faithfulness, commitment, obedience, love, and determination, Ruth ended up marrying Boaz and providing him with a son (and Naomi with a grandson) named Obed, who became the grandfather of David and an ancestor of Jesus.

May we have this kind of loving relationship with Jesus that Ruth had with Naomi! He has given us everything, and He asks for us to be wholly surrendered to Him in return. Might we have the same type of measureless devotion to Him that He displayed for us on the cross.

Perhaps at Jesus' call for utter abandonment to Him, you shrink back. It seems too risky, too difficult, too scary for you to give Him all He asks. You see others going through this life without even acknowledging His presence, and they seem to be getting along just fine. So why must you surrender yourself to the nth degree to this Son of God called Jesus?

Although you do not yet know it, when you surrender yourself to Christ and obey Him in everything, you will be fulfilling your spiritual destiny. In wholly binding your life to Him, you will discover the reality of the Almighty God! You will be walking in light, not darkness. You will have such an intimate relationship with the Creator that He will tell you things those who are further away from Him do not know! All you need to do is be totally obedient to Him, to the point where like the psalmist you will declare, "I delight to do thy will, O my God" (Psalm 40:8 KJV).

This privilege of surrender is one that is not demanded by God. It is a matter of our choice, part of our free will. In her travels, Smith came across the quote, "Perfect obedience would be perfect happiness, if only we had perfect confidence in the power we were obeying." Do you have that perfect confidence to totally abandon yourself to God and be perfectly obedient? If so, nothing can keep you from having the perfect joy of the Lord, for Jesus has said, "Blessed (happy and to be envied) rather are those who hear the Word of God and obey and practice it!" (Luke 11:28 AMP).

If we obey (or keep) His commands, we prove our love for Him. In return, Christ will not only love what we're doing but will show Himself to us. The

Amplified Bible says it this way:

> *The person who has My commands and keeps them is the one who [really]*
> *loves Me; and whoever [really] loves Me will be loved by My Father, and I*
> *[too] will love him and will show (reveal, manifest) Myself to him. [I will let*
> *Myself be clearly seen by him and make Myself real to him.] (John 14:21)*

Jesus makes this offer of an intimate, loving, revelatory relationship to all who will
say yes to Him, but all do not accept His invitation. Other interests and loves (of
others or self) are too precious for them to cast aside. The future of heaven is still
available to them, but they will miss out on the unfathomable joy of this present
moment!

How wonderful that Jesus so desires us to rely on Him instead of ourselves.
Smith writes:

> *That we should need Him is easy to comprehend; that He should need*
> *us seems incomprehensible. That our desire should be toward Him*
> *is a matter of course; but that His desire should be toward us passes*
> *the bounds of human belief. And yet He says it, and what can we do*
> *but believe Him? He has made our hearts capable of this supreme*
> *overmastering affection and has offered Himself as the object of it. It is*
> *infinitely precious to Him. So much does He value it, that He has made*
> *it the first and chiefest of all His commandments that we should love*
> *Him with all our might, and with all our strength. Continually at every*
> *heart He is knocking, asking to be taken in as the supreme object of love.*
> *(Emphasis in original)*

And when we do, we will be like women who have built their houses not upon the
sand but upon Jesus—the Rock of ages. With Him as our foundation, as we obey
Him and His Word every moment of every day, we will be able to keep our heads
in times of temptation or persecution. We will keep our comfort, hope, peace,

and joy in the midst of distressing situations; and we will be kept spurred on by His amazing power! When we keep on obeying Him, He will keep us safe, strong, resilient, and joyful all through our lives.

A mother trains up her child to obey her. When a child asks *why*, she merely says, "Because, I said so." God would train us the same way. And not only are we instructed to obey God and His commands diligently, but we are to meditate on them. For if we do not bathe ourselves in His Word, we will perhaps be unclear as to what He wants us to do. And the more we look to God for answers, the more we will begin to see everything through His eyes 24–7 and keep ourselves from immediately looking to others, or ourselves, for direction.

If only our desire to chase after Him would be as great as our desire for a new pair of shoes or a purse! If you do not yet have that desire, pray that God would grant you passion for His Word, understanding of His love, and a yearning to follow Him with everything you are.

For God's insights will be revealed to you the moment you obey:

Abruptly Jesus broke into prayer: "Thank you, Father, Lord of heaven and earth. You've concealed your ways from sophisticates and know-it-alls, but spelled them out clearly to ordinary people. Yes, Father, that's the way you like to work." (Matthew 11:25 MSG)

May we, too, abruptly break into prayer when God speaks to us, ordinary people, and through our obedience does extraordinary things, not just in our lives but in the lives of others. We need not understand what He is doing or why, merely faithfully step out in obedience. Instantly, the next door opens, the sea parts, or the ram appears.

In this loving relationship with Christ, God may at times be silent. This is a sign of the intimacy we have with Him, like an old couple who sit quietly together, at times, comfortable in each other's silent presence. This may be a moment in which we must patiently await His next message, content with remaining with Him and meditating on His Word. For if we run ahead, uncertain of His will, we may miss the miracle He is about to perform. "When He heard that he [Lazarus] was sick, He stayed two more days in the place where He was" (John 11:6 NKJV). Only later did Jesus raise him.

Your love and devotion are all the Lord asks of you as a reward for all He has done for you. So give Him everything you are! Smith writes:

Lay your whole life open before Him that He may control it. Say to Him each day, "Lord, enable me to regulate this day so as to please you! Give me spiritual insight to discover what is your will in all the relations of my life. Guide me as to my pursuits, my friendships, my reading, my dress, my Christian work." Do not let there be a day nor an hour in which you are not consciously doing His will and following Him wholly.

Consciously recognize God's presence in everything and you will be brimming over with joy as you reap the blessings of hearing His will—and keeping it.

Restore the joy of your salvation to me,
and provide me with a spirit of willing obedience.
PSALM 51:12 GW

$\mathscr{P}$ATH MARKERS

$\mathscr{P}$romise

"This is what I commanded them, saying, 'Obey My voice, and I will be your God, and you shall be My people. And walk in all the ways that I have commanded you, that it may be well with you.' "

JEREMIAH 7:23 NKJV

$\mathscr{P}$roof

During the forty days after he suffered and died, he [Jesus] appeared to the apostles from time to time, and he proved to them in many ways that he was actually alive. And he talked to them about the Kingdom of God.

Once when he was eating with them, he commanded them, "Do not leave Jerusalem until the Father sends you the gift he promised, as I told you before. John baptized with water, but in just a few days you will be baptized with the Holy Spirit." . . .

On the day of Pentecost all the believers were meeting together in one place. Suddenly, there was a sound from heaven like the roaring of a mighty windstorm, and it filled the house where they were sitting. Then, what looked like flames or tongues of fire appeared and settled on each of them. And everyone present was filled with the Holy Spirit and began speaking in other languages, as the Holy Spirit gave them this ability.

ACTS 1:3–5; 2:1–4 NLT

$\mathscr{P}$rovision

Continue to work out your salvation with fear and trembling. It is God who produces in you the desires and actions that please him.

PHILIPPIANS 2:12–13 GW

Portrait

In Christ, I am loved by God and delight to do His will (see John 14:21).

Mind-Renewing Prayers

Day 1
A Perfect Turnout

*And we know that all things work together for good to those who
love God, to those who are the called according to His purpose.*
ROMANS 8:28 NKJV

*Although I may not understand my current situation, I know that all things
will work out for my good. Why? Because that's what You have promised me.
You have a purpose for me. So I will continue to obey You, Lord, knowing all
will turn out well in the end. Because I have confidence in You, Your ways,
and Your timing, I have peace. This is the only way to live.*

Day 2
Moment-to-Moment Surrender

As a young man marries a young woman, so will your Builder marry you;
as a bridegroom rejoices over his bride, so will your God rejoice over you.
Isaiah 62:5 tniv

I feel so unworthy for You to rejoice over me! But that's what Your Word says.
As I love and find amazing delight in my own child, so You love and find
amazing delight in me. So I am walking in Your path, Lord. I'm keeping my
eyes on the road You have laid out before me. Moment to moment I surrender
to You all that I am—and all that I have.

Day 3
From the Ground Up

"And all these blessings shall come upon you and overtake you,
because you obey the voice of the Lord your God."
Deuteronomy 28:2 nkjv

I can't imagine blessings overtaking me, but that's what You have promised.
And all because I am obeying You. Keep speaking to me, Lord. My ears are
open to Your commands. My eyes are open to the Way explained in Your Word.
My heart is open to Your love and affection. My mind is open to Your vision for
me. I am building my life in You from the ground up.

Day 4
Commands to Love

You shall love the Lord your God out of and with your whole heart and out of and with all your soul (your life) and out of and with all your mind (with your faculty of thought and your moral understanding) and out of and with all your strength. This is the first and principal commandment. The second is like it and is this, You shall love your neighbor as yourself. There is no other commandment greater than these.
MARK 12:30–31 AMP

Lord, your commands to love are what I'm determined to obey. I'm resolved to love You with not just any love, but a strong, deep, thrilling, enduring, and passionate love that truly connects me with You. Harder is the love for myself and my "neighbor." Help me to like myself more—and to be as loving and patient with others as You are with me.

Day 5
Running After You

By faith, Noah built a ship in the middle of dry land. He was warned about something he couldn't see, and acted on what he was told. The result? His family was saved. His act of faith drew a sharp line between the evil of the unbelieving world and the rightness of the believing world. As a result, Noah became intimate with God.
HEBREWS 11:7 MSG

I want to be as intimate with You as Noah was, Lord. I want to be as determined and dedicated a follower after You as Ruth. I know that by doing so I may be leaving behind the world I knew. But I'd rather be running after You than staying where I am. So show me the way, Lord. Light the fire of obedience within my heart, mind, body, and soul. Save me with obedient faith.

Day 6
Endless Source

*Oh, how I love your law! I meditate on it all day long. Your commands are
always with me and make me wiser than my enemies. I have more insight than
all my teachers, for I meditate on your statutes. I have more understanding
than the elders, for I obey your precepts.*
PSALM 119:97–100 TNIV

*I crave Your Word, Lord. I love lingering in it, allowing it to permeate my very
being. When You reveal Yourself to me, I glean such wonderful insights. Your
Word not only gladdens my heart but boosts my spirit, nourishes my soul,
and lights my pathway. Thank You for providing me with this endless source of
wisdom.*

Day 7
The Open Door

*Your written instructions are miraculous. That is why I obey them.
Your word is a doorway that lets in light, and it helps gullible people understand.
I open my mouth and pant because I long for your commandments.*
PSALM 119:129–131 GW

*Just when I feel as if I am lost in a fog, I find the open door to understanding in
Your Word. To me, Your manual for life is something I cannot live without. For
each page speaks of Your presence. Each word draws me closer to You. Each verse
finds a home in my heart. Continue to open my eyes, Lord. Give me the vision I
need to follow You from one door to another.*

PART 4:

The Grand Mother

You have seen what I did to the Egyptians,
and how I bore you on eagles' wings
and brought you to Myself.

EXODUS 19:4 AMP

Chapter 18
The Princess and the Peace of Divine Union

[Christiana said,] The Prince of the place has also sent for me,
with promise of [receiving me] if I shall come to Him. . . .
O Thou loving One! O Thou blessed One! Thou deservest to have me;
Thou hast bought me; Thou deservest to have me all.
John Bunyan, *The Pilgrim's Progress: Part 2*

• • • • • • •

While growing up, we read fairy tales about beautiful princesses who met or were rescued by princes, fell in love, and lived happily ever after. Yet later, if we ourselves married, we discovered that although we loved our spouses, they were far from the ideal prince. And if we will be honest with ourselves, we were far from being princesses—especially when the time came for giving birth to the heir apparent.

But here's the really good part. When we become Christians, we have a chance of actually *fulfilling* the happily-ever-after fairy tale with the one and only true Prince—Jesus Christ. He is the One who can rescue us from the poverty of ashes and the tower of temptation. With His kiss, we are awakened to a new reality. On Him alone can we rely, for He will never leave us. He is our comfort, peace, and rock. *He* is the One with whom we want to become one and live happily ever after.

"Before the foundation of the world" (1 Peter 1:20 NASB), God's plan was for our souls and spirits to be united with our ultimate bridegroom. This divine union is what Jesus prayed for—and not just for His disciples but for us, those who would later come to believe in Him (see John 17:21). This union was the "mystery which has been hidden from ages and from generations, but now has been revealed" (Colossians 1:26 NKJV), was disclosed through the scriptures, and "is made known to all nations" (Romans 16:26 AMP). Because of Christ's death, we are right with God and can be united with Him (see Romans 10:4).

God has not made our union with Him difficult, nor has He kept it a secret. Yet some of us may not yet completely grasp the concept of being fully one with God. Perhaps our hearts do not fully believe it is available to us. Or we may be afraid to trust Him totally. Yet that is where this entire pathway of Christian life is leading to—*voluntarily* embracing a oneness with God. He will not be satisfied until our spirits and souls have reached their destiny of a divine union with Him (see Isaiah 53:11).

The usual path of Christians may mirror that of the first twelve disciples. Jesus called them, awakening them to their need of Him. They looked up and immediately left their old lives to follow Him. Hearing His message, they believed. They worked for Him, talked with Him, walked with Him. But they were still so different from Him. They argued about who would be the greatest. Many times, they misunderstood His messages. At the end, all but one of the men ran from the cross. Jesus still had sent them out to spread His message with their words and actions, empowering them to heal the sick—physically, emotionally, mentally, and spiritually.

That seems to cover the behavior of the male disciples. So what about our foremothers? What was their path like? In *The Pilgrim's Progress: Part 2*, John Bunyan describes the roles of Jesus' female followers:

> *When the Saviour was come, women rejoiced in Him before either man or angel (Luke 2). I read not, that ever any man did give unto Christ so much as one groat; but the women followed Him, and ministered to Him of their substance (Luke 8:2, 3). It was a woman that washed His feet with tears, and a woman that anointed His body to the burial (Luke 7:37, 50; John 11:2; 12:3). They were women that wept, when He was going to the Cross, and women that followed Him from the Cross, and that sat by His sepulchre, when he was buried (Luke 23:27; Matt. 27:55, 56, 61). They were women that were first with Him at His resurrection-morn; and women that brought tidings first to His disciples, that He was risen from the dead (Luke 24:22, 23). Women, therefore, are highly favoured.*

This reads as if women were quietly going about the duty of patiently serving, loving, nurturing, and following Jesus, content to simply stay in the background of the then largely male-dominated society, except for their role in the *fore*front during the birth and resurrection announcements. Yes, women definitely stuck with Jesus—through thick and thin, through celebration *and* crucifixion.

But in the end, both men *and* women cowered together in a locked room, wondering how they would survive the coming days. All of Jesus' followers had known only the physical Christ as someone apart from them, their Teacher and Master. What would they do now? The only thing they could do. Continue to trust in Jesus, His words, and God's promises: "I will send the Holy Spirit upon you, just as my Father promised. Don't begin telling others yet—stay here in the city until the Holy Spirit comes and fills you with power from heaven" (Luke 24:49 TLB).

Later, while in that upper room in Jerusalem, "without warning there was a sound like a strong wind, gale force—no one could tell where it came from. It filled the whole building. Then, like a wildfire, the Holy Spirit spread through their ranks" (Acts 2:2–4 MSG)! It was then—without warning—that the disciples were filled with Christ within! There was no parting from Him now! They were one with Christ, filled with and aware of His life, Spirit, and power within them.

Perhaps you have traveled this same path. You believe that Christ existed— that He was the Father's answer to our final reconciliation with Him. You have confidence that He loves you, that He is beside You and will walk with you through storm and fire, yet you have not given yourself totally to Him but are holding back. Perhaps your will and His are not yet fully joined. Smith writes:

> *You have not yet lost your own life that you may live only in His. Once it was "I and not Christ." Next it was "I and Christ." Perhaps now it is even "Christ and I." But has it come yet to be Christ only, and not I at all?*

This miraculous union of our hearts and Christ's, planned since the beginning of time, is meant for us all. In fact, it happened when you accepted Christ. First Corinthians 3:16 tell us: "You realize, don't you, that you are the temple of God, and God himself is present in you? No one will get by with vandalizing God's temple, you can be sure of that. God's temple is sacred—and you, remember, are the temple" (MSG). Dwelling within you, a true believer, is the Spirit of Christ. And if you read to whom this applies, you'll see that this scripture pertains to "mere infants [in the new life] in Christ" (1 Corinthians 3:1 AMP) who are still being fed with milk! Thus this is not a new dimension to your life as a believer. Christ has been residing in you all along! You have *already been* transformed into a new creature—and *already are* a temple of the living God! Smith writes:

> *Although this is true, it is also equally true that unless the believer knows it and lives in the power of it, it is to him as though it were not. Like the treasures under a man's field, which existed there before they were known or used by him, so does the life of Christ dwell in each believer as really before he knows it and lives in it as it does afterward; although its power is not manifested until, intelligently and voluntarily, the believer ceases from his own life and accepts Christ's life in its place.*

As soon as you accept this divine blending as a reality and devise to give up self, the power of oneness with God manifests itself!

When we consciously and consistently recognize Christ within and truly, fully, and intimately are one with Christ, we are impelled "to live the same kind of life Jesus lived" (1 John 2:6 MSG). That means walking the walk and talking the talk. It means giving Christ not partial but full reign, complete control: "You are living the life of the Spirit, if the [Holy] Spirit of God [really] dwells within you [directs and controls you]" (Romans 8:9 AMP). It means being spent in love for others as Christ spent Himself in love for us (see John 21:17). It means feeding His sheep, for He has told us, "As my Father hath sent me, even so send I you" (John 20:21 KJV).

Living in the full power of a union with Christ, you will exhibit a change in character. Your nature will become loving, joyful, peaceful, long-suffering, kind, good, faithful, gentle, and self-controlled (see Galatians 5:22–23). Because you are fully aware that He is living through you, you won't be able to be anything but, for you have become "partakers of the divine nature" (2 Peter 1:4 NASB). Because He is holy, you will be holy.

And it's not only your character that reveals you have become united with Christ. The things you do will also be a testament to the truth of your divine union (see John 5:19; 10:38).

This truth will be evident regardless of your emotions on a certain day. Smith says:

> *Pay no regard to your feelings, therefore, in this oneness with Christ, but see to it that you have the really vital fruits of a oneness in character and walk and mind. Your emotions may be very delightful, or they may be very depressing. In neither case are they any real indications of your spiritual state. . . .Your joy in the Lord is to be a far deeper thing than a mere emotion. It is to be the joy of knowledge, of perception, of actual existence.*

How wonderful to have a joy that is not tied to what happens to us throughout our days, especially in those early years of motherhood, from birth to late teens. Regardless of whether or not our child is sick, misbehaving, hanging with the wrong crowd, or any other of those gray hair–raising dilemmas, we can have deep, abiding joy because we are trusting in Jesus, His Word, and God's promises of this divine union. Knowing that Christ is loving us within and sheltering us without, that no one can truly harm us, is contentment at its best.

It's also wonderful that our God never forces Himself upon us. Instead, He wants us to *come to Him willingly*. We are already God's living temple. Christ already resides in us, and we already received the Holy Spirit when we accepted Christ. What we need to do is to continually, consistently, and completely *recognize* Christ's presence within us and *surrender* ourselves to Him.

Although you have known Christ is in you, at times you may have ignored His presence, either through fear or disinterestedness or simply because you were too caught up in the thrills and spills of motherhood and life in general. Perhaps there have been times you felt unprepared for Him, or perhaps you did not want Him to see the real you, so to save yourself embarrassment, you've kept Him at arm's length. While doing so, you have missed out on the full peace, power, protection, guidance, insights, and other valuable treasures He could have bestowed upon you and your life! Be at peace. He has already seen all that you are and all that you do—and loves you unconditionally!

So do not fear. Christ has been with you all along. He is ready to help you rest in Him. Allow Him to carry all your burdens, give you insights only He would have, and empower you to live your life to the fullest 24–7. This is what you have been created for, for it is not you who lives but Christ lives in you.

Because our partaking of the divine nature is not forced upon us but is something we volunteer to do, we must give our Prince a willing yes every minute of every day or the joy of our full and wonderful union with Him will be left wanting. Thus we are to follow the four *A*'s of abiding:

1. *Acknowledge* our oneness with Christ—it's a real thing.
2. *Abdicate* our throne—our will, mind, body, spirit, and soul are now fully His, not ours.
3. *Allow* Him to take *total* possession of us—no part of us is left behind.
4. *Affirm* firmly that He *has*, indeed, taken possession of, is dwelling with, and has complete control of us—it is no longer we who live but Christ who is living in us.

By surrendering all to Christ, we will possess nothing—and thereby everything! For He is all we truly need. Fully recognizing, acknowledging, and enjoying our union with Christ, we and our Prince—along with our little heirs to the throne—can live together happily ever after, with no end in sight!

All day and night, may we steadfastly rely on and trust in Jesus, each knowing for certain this truth: Christ lives in me.

I have been crucified with Christ. My ego is no longer central. . . .
I am no longer driven to impress God. Christ lives in me.
GALATIANS 2:20 MSG

PATH MARKERS

Promise

Whoever obeys what Christ says is the kind of person in whom God's love is perfected. That's how we know we are in Christ. Those who say that they live in him must live the same way he lived.

1 JOHN 2:5–6 GW

Proof

[Jesus prayed,] I tell you, if anyone steadfastly believes in Me, he will himself be able to do the things that I do; and he will do even greater things than these, because I go to the Father. . . .

Neither for these. . .alone do I pray [it is not for their sake only that I make this request], but also for all those who will ever come to believe in Me through their word and teaching, that they all may be one, [just] as You, Father, are in Me and I in You, that they also may be one in Us, so that the world may believe and be convinced that You have sent Me. . . .

Now as Peter went here and there among them all, he went down also to the saints who lived at Lydda. There he found a man named Aeneas, who had been bedfast for eight years and was paralyzed. And Peter said to him, Aeneas, Jesus Christ (the Messiah) [now] makes you whole. Get up and make your bed! And immediately [Aeneas] stood up. Then all the inhabitants of Lydda and the plain of Sharon saw [what had happened to] him and they turned to the Lord.

JOHN 14:12; 17:20–21; ACTS 9:32–35 AMP

Provision

Through his glory and integrity he has given us his promises that are of the highest value. Through these promises you will share in the divine nature because you have escaped the corruption that sinful desires cause in the world.

2 PETER 1:4 GW

Portrait

In Christ, I am spiritually blessed because He lives in me (see Ephesians 1:3).

MIND-RENEWING PRAYERS

DAY 1
An Awesome, Miraculous Gift

You surely know that your body is a temple where the Holy Spirit lives. The Spirit is in you and is a gift from God. You are no longer your own.

1 CORINTHIANS 6:19 CEV

Lord, it's hard to believe my body is a sacred place, a place where Your Spirit resides. But that's what Your Word says—so I'm taking it as a major truth! Help me to keep Your temple as a vehicle fit for Your use—and view it as an awesome, miraculous gift that only You could design, maintain, and rule!

DAY 2
Beloved Prince

I have died, but Christ lives in me. And I now live by faith
in the Son of God, who loved me and gave his life for me.
GALATIANS 2:20 CEV

Oh, how my ego loves to be in charge! But that is not how You want it to be. So,
Lord, I acknowledge my oneness with You. My "I" is stepping aside, abdicating
its throne. I allow you to take full and total possession of all that I am. And
I affirm that You, my beloved Prince, are the one now living in me, happily
ever after.

DAY 3
Abide Fully

The spiritual nature produces love, joy, peace, patience,
kindness, goodness, faithfulness, gentleness, and self-control.
GALATIANS 5:22–23 GW

Since allowing You to abide in me, things are changing, Lord. It's no longer
all about me—but about You and others. This Spirit life is turning my world
upside down but in a good way. Thank You for taking over the reins of my life
and making me a better mom in so many ways. Continue to remind me each
day to live Your way and bear Your fruit.

Day 4

"Yes, Lord, Yes!"

You are living the life of the Spirit, if the [Holy] Spirit of God
[really] dwells within you [directs and controls you].
ROMANS 8:9 AMP

Some days it isn't easy, Lord. It's a continuous, "Yes, Lord, yes," that needs to
come off my lips. So keep me surrendered to You, for when I give You complete
control, I have so much deep joy. And things just seem to go better when I'm
trusting in You—not me. So here I am again today, Lord, saying, "Yes, Lord,
yes!" Rule me! Take me! I'm Yours!

Day 5

From the Inside Out

Put on the new self, which in the likeness of God has
been created in righteousness and holiness of the truth.
EPHESIANS 4:24 NASB

Every day when I open my closet, trying to figure out what to wear, I'm
reminded I'm to put on my new self. I want a God-fashioned life, one that is
created in Your image. Your dream for me from the beginning was just to
trust You and believe in Your promises. So that's what I'm doing today, Lord.
Clothing myself in You, changing, living, and loving from the inside out!

Day 6
Christ-Centered Self

*But whoever obeys what Christ says is the kind of person in
whom God's love is perfected. That's how we know we are in Christ.*
1 John 2:5 gw

When I recognize Your presence within me, Jesus, I cannot help but be
overwhelmed with Your love. And when I am in that love, I know I am being
my true self, my Christ-centered self. Thank You for giving me this eternal light
and life. Thank You for dying so that I could truly live.

Day 7
Divine Union

*All praise to God, the Father of our Lord Jesus Christ,
who has blessed us with every spiritual blessing in the
heavenly realms because we are united with Christ.*
Ephesians 1:3 nlt

Sometimes it seems so hard to believe that You have been thinking about me
since the beginning of time. That You have loved me from day one. That Your
plan has been to continually draw me ever closer to You and Your vision for
my life. Thank You, Father God, for the blessing that is Jesus and enabling me
to experience a divine union with Him.

CHAPTER 19
The Charioteer and Her Transport

Behold, all the banks beyond the river were full of horses and chariots,
which were come down from above to accompany [Christiana] to the city gate.
JOHN BUNYAN, *THE PILGRIM'S PROGRESS: PART 2*

• • • • • • •

*H*annah Whitall Smith had a unique perspective on the problems and trials we encounter in this earthly life, declaring that "they are God's chariots, sent to take the soul to its high places of triumph." But how can that be, for often our earthly woes don't seem to resemble God's chariots at all? Instead, our mortal miseries manifest themselves as fears, stresses, heartaches, disputes, trials, offenses, misunderstandings, losses, and callousness. They are like juggernauts,[1] steamrollers that wound and crush our spirits, poised to roll right over us and sink us down mercilessly into the earth. Yet it's all just a matter of perception. For if we could see these woes as God's vehicles of victory, we would rise above our cares in triumph, attaining heights we never dreamed possible! The juggernaut is the tangible, visible, earthly conveyance, whereas the chariot of God is the intangible, invisible vehicle that will take us to the heavenly places.

One morning, the servant of the prophet Elisha went outside in Dothan and became alarmed when he saw the king of Syria's army of horses and chariots surrounding the city. He asked Elisha, "Alas, my master! What shall we do?" (2 Kings 6:15 NKJV). Elisha answered:

> *"Do not fear, for those who are with us are more than those who are with them." And Elisha prayed, and said, "LORD, I pray, open his eyes that he may see." Then the LORD opened the eyes of the young man, and he*

saw. And behold, the mountain was full of horses and chariots of fire all around Elisha. (2 Kings 6:16–17 NKJV)

Would that we would also see our worldly woes with spiritual vision, that we would open our eyes to the invisible powers of God that come to our rescue! Such "eyesight" would allow us to rise above our juggernauts in God's chariots, into the "heavenly places in Christ Jesus" (Ephesians 2:6 KJV) where victory over everything below would be ours!

Like Elisha, we have a choice. We can walk by faith, not by sight. We can allow our juggernauts—big or little—to crush us, plunging us down into fear, defeat, and despair, or we can jump into the chariots of God and rise above them in triumph. And it doesn't matter what or how many are our worldly woes. What matters is how we take them!

All the losses, trials, minor irritations, worries, and woes that come to us become chariots the moment we treat them as such. Smith writes:

> *Whenever we mount into God's chariots the same thing happens to us spiritually that happened to Elijah. We shall have a translation. Not into the heavens above us, as Elijah did, but into the heaven within us; and this, after all, is almost a grander translation than his. We shall be carried away from the low, earthly groveling plane of life, where everything hurts and everything is unhappy, up into the "heavenly places in Christ Jesus" [Ephesians 2:6 KJV], where we can ride in triumph over all below.*
>
> *These "heavenly places" are interior, not exterior; and the road that leads to them is interior also. But the chariot that carries the soul over this road is generally some outward loss or trial or disappointment; some chastening that does not indeed seem for the present to be joyous, but grievous; but that nevertheless afterward "yieldeth the peaceable fruit of righteousness" [Hebrews 12:11 KJV.]*

So what steps can we take when, like Elisha's servant, we cry out, "Alas, my master! What shall we do?" (2 Kings 6:15 NKJV), when we have conflicts without and fears within (see 2 Corinthians 7:5)? First, we need to *quiet ourselves by word*. We need to tell ourselves, "Do not fear, for those who are with us are more than those who are with them" (2 Kings 6:16 NKJV). No matter what comes against us—to destroy, offend, or frighten us—God is infinitely more powerful. When we are magnifying the causes of our fear, we need to take hold of ourselves with clear, direct, great, inspiring thoughts of God and His invisible, intangible world. "We know that in all things God works for the good of those who love him. He appointed them to be saved in keeping with his purpose. . . . Since God is on our side, who can be against us?" (Romans 8:28, 31 NIrV). We also know that "God is our place of safety. He gives us strength. He is always there to help us in times of trouble" (Psalm 46:1 NIrV).

Then we must *quiet ourselves by vision*. Elisha prayed for his servant, "LORD, I pray, open his eyes that he may see" (2 Kings 6:17 NKJV). The servant's eyes of faith were opened to God's multitude of chariots! This is the prayer we must pray for ourselves. Once our spiritual vision is twenty-twenty, the darkness will dissipate and we will see and believe the power of heaven. The dangers of earth and the fear that arises from them will vanish as the darkness before us, allowing us to be carried into the heavenly places in our chariots "paved with love" (Song of Solomon 3:10 KJV).

In the temporal world, our chariots don't seem like they are paved with love. Instead, they often appear very unattractive. Our chariots may be the sickness of our children or the rebelliousness of our teens. It may be the job we, as sole providers, have just lost. It could be the death of a loved one or a major disappointment when our dreams suddenly seem unattainable. Or the cruelties of neglect, greed, malice, and selfishness practiced in the world. Yet every chariot sent by God (whether of first or second cause) must be paved with love, for our "God is love" (1 John 4:8 KJV).

Habakkuk says God rides upon horses and chariots "of victory and deliverance" (3:8 AMP). Psalm 68:33 says God "rides upon the highest heavens" (NASB). "He makes the clouds His chariot; He walks upon the wings of the wind" (Psalm 104:3 NASB). In His majesty, He rides "prosperously because of truth and meekness and righteousness" (Psalm 45:4 KJV). Thus we must look to God and His chariots to carry us over the trials and tribulations, torments and troubles of this tangible world.

We will not prosper if we look to an earthly conveyance to help us through, for God has told us, "Woe to them that go down to Egypt for help; and stay on horses, and trust in chariots" (Isaiah 31:1 KJV). Our "Egypt" consists of tangible resources we can see. We find ourselves tempted to rely on them because they look real and dependable, whereas God's chariots are intangible and invisible, not seen except by faith. Going "down to Egypt for help" may be depending on money alone to make us feel secure or to make our children happy. It may be the counsel of a friend or the wisdom of a husband that we've come to lean on more than God. It may be the favorite preacher we believe we can't live without or we will weaken, then die, for lack of spiritual strength.

Remember Ichabod's mother—wife of the immoral priest named Phinehas, daughter-in-law of the indulgent parent and priest named Eli? At hearing the news of the death of her husband and father-in-law, as well as the capture of the ark of the covenant, she went into early labor. After the midwives told her, "Fear not; for thou hast born a son" (1 Samuel 4:20 KJV), she named him Ichabod, meaning, "The glory is departed from Israel: because the ark of God was taken" (1 Samuel 4:21 KJV). Apparently, Ichabod's mom had more faith in the ark of God than in God Himself! Instead of riding in God's chariot when faced with death and the loss of God's ark, she allowed an earthly juggernaut to steamroll her with hopelessness and despair, which led to her untimely demise.

Anything we rely on other than God will, at some point, be taken away. Smith writes, "God is obliged often to destroy all our own earthly chariots before He can bring us to the point of mounting into His." He longs to have us depend on Him more than anything or anyone else. For He was, is, and will be the only one we *can* truly depend on. History proves it. "In the wilderness. . .you saw how the LORD your God carried you, as a father carries his son, all the way you went until you reached this place" (Deuteronomy 1:31 TNIV).

Lot's wife favored, depended on, and was linked more to her material possessions and worldly status than God. She attempted to escape her juggernaut, but the lure of the world trapped her on the way to her chariot of God.

Leah seems definitely to have been a charioteer. Her apparently weak eyesight and plainness, worldly deficits, changed her inwardly, helping her to become more spiritually aware. The fact that her husband so obviously loved her sister Rachel more than Leah drove the latter to ride in another chariot, where she learned to be content amid grief and trial. All these chariots that led to Leah's depending more on God than all else carried her to victory inwardly—and ultimately outwardly! For she was blessed not only by birthing six sons but also by outliving her sister, Rachel, which enabled Leah to finally have Jacob all to herself!

Joseph had a vision of his future victories and reign, but the chariots that took him there—being betrayed by his brothers, sold as a slave, falsely accused of rape, and then imprisoned—looked more like juggernauts of agony and failure. Yet because God and His chariots were with him, giving him strength and courage, he did not get discouraged but rose above his earthly cares, even while in a dungeon. Joseph's earthly travails were a strange route to becoming a ruler of Egypt and saving himself and his family, but he could not have gotten there any other way. In the same regard, our road to the heavenly mansion that awaits us is often reached by similar chariots.

Do not allow the juggernauts of this world to roll over you and sink you into the pits of despair, desperation, and fear. Do not follow in the footsteps of Ichabod's mom or Lot's wife. Instead, be like Leah, Ruth, Hannah, Elizabeth, and Mary, the mother of Jesus. Exile your ego, and embrace the spirit of service. Mount up with God, taking each offense, bitter word, tragedy, loss, trial, and temptation as your chariot of God that will take you to the "heavenly places in Christ Jesus" (Ephesians 2:6 KJV). Take the Lord's road and forget every external obstacle, knowing God has established your steps (see Psalm 40:2). In doing so, you cannot help but triumph.

Become like Paul, whose "thorn in the flesh" and losses were nothing compared to the richness he found in gaining Christ (see Philippians 3:7–9). Instead of allowing worldly woes to cast him down, Paul "[ascribed] strength to God," whose "strength is in the clouds" (Psalm 68:34 NKJV).

Before you may have been blind, but now like Elisha's servant, you see the mighty chariots of God. Take each juggernaut event in your life—big or little—and gird yourself in the Word, open your spiritual eyes, and board the chariot for your soul. Smith writes:

When your trial comes, then, put it right into the will of God and climb into that will as a little child climbs into its mother's arms. The baby carried in the chariot of its mother's arms rides triumphantly through the hardest places and does not even know they are hard. And how much more we, who are carried in the chariot of the "arms of God"! . . .

You must not be half-hearted about it. You must climb wholly into your chariot, not with one foot dragging on the ground. . . . You must accept God's will fully, and must hide yourself in the arms of His love, that are always underneath to receive you, in every circumstance and at every moment. Say, "Thy will be done, Thy will be done," over and over.

When faced with trials, quiet yourself with God's Word and vision. Know that He is working out all things for your good. Ask Him to open Your eyes. Then allow your chariot to take you to the heavenly places where you can "ride prosperously" (Psalm 45:4 NKJV) with God on top of all, empowering you, allowing you to triumph within and without!

The Lord gives the word [of power]; the women who bear and publish [the news] are a great host.
PSALM 68:11 AMP

$\mathcal{P}$ATH MARKERS

$\mathcal{P}$romise

The chariots of God are twenty thousand, even thousands of thousands. . . .
Blessed be the Lord, who daily loads us with benefits, the God of our salvation!
. . . His strength is in the clouds. O God, You are more awesome than Your holy
places. The God of Israel is He who gives strength and power to His people.

PSALM 68:17, 19, 34–35 NKJV

$\mathcal{P}$roof

Therefore, since we have this ministry, as we have received mercy, we do not
lose heart. . . . Since we have the same spirit of faith, according to what is
written, "I believed and therefore I spoke," we also believe and therefore speak,
knowing that He who raised up the Lord Jesus will also raise us up with Jesus,
and will present us with you. For all things are for your sakes, that grace,
having spread through the many, may cause thanksgiving to abound to the
glory of God. Therefore we do not lose heart. Even though our outward man
is perishing, yet the inward man is being renewed day by day. For our light
affliction, which is but for a moment, is working for us a far more exceeding
and eternal weight of glory, while we do not look at the things which are
seen, but at the things which are not seen. For the things which are seen are
temporary, but the things which are not seen are eternal. . . . I know a man in
Christ who fourteen years ago—whether in the body I do not know, or whether
out of the body I do not know, God knows—such a one was caught up to the
third heaven. And I know such a man—whether in the body or out of the body
I do not know, God knows—how he was caught up into Paradise.

2 CORINTHIANS 4:1, 13–18; 12:2–4 NKJV

Provision

All praise to God, the Father of our Lord Jesus Christ, who has blessed us with every spiritual blessing in the heavenly realms because we are united with Christ.

EPHESIANS 1:3 NLT

Portrait

In Christ, I am raised to new life, setting my eyes on the realities of heaven (see Colossians 3:1).

MIND-RENEWING PRAYERS

DAY 1
Climbing Up!

Since you have been raised to new life with Christ, set your sights on the realities of heaven, where Christ sits in the place of honor at God's right hand.

COLOSSIANS 3:1 NLT

I'm keeping my eyes on You, Lord. I know what is true, what is reality. All the cares of this world, heavy though they may be, are not for me to bear. So I am climbing up into Your chariot, knowing that all things will work out for good, and that You are riding with me all the way!

DAY 2
Into God's Arms

*"In the wilderness. . .you saw how the LORD your God carried you,
as a father carries his son, all the way you went until you reached this place."*
DEUTERONOMY 1:31 TNIV

*Sometimes, Lord, I feel so low. I feel as if I cannot move, for so many burdens
are keeping me down. My hopes and dreams for myself and my children seem
untenable. But I don't want all these woes to bury me, Lord. Help me to rise
up, to crawl, then walk, then run into Your arms. Carry me to Your chariot,
where I know I will be safe and will triumph!*

DAY 3
Open Eyes

*"Don't be afraid!" Elisha told him. "For there are more on our side than
on theirs!" Then Elisha prayed, "O LORD, open his eyes and let him see!"
The LORD opened the young man's eyes, and when he looked up,
he saw that the hillside around Elisha was filled with horses and chariots of fire.*
2 KINGS 6:16–17 NLT

*I'm tired of giving in to my fears. This is no way to live the life You have given
me! So right now, in this very moment, I am praying, Lord: Open my eyes! Let
me see Your chariots surrounding me! Show me the victory I have in following
Your ways. Help me to stop dragging my feet. I'm committing to Your chariot,
Lord. Help me ride with the wind!*

DAY 4
So Far Above

O LORD my God, You are very great. . . . He makes the
clouds His chariot. He walks upon the wings of the wind.
PSALM 104:1, 3 NASB

You are so far above all trials and tribulations of this earth. You have that
infinite space and time perspective, that God's-eye view that makes what seems
to matter today of no consequence tomorrow. And I know You want to grow
me into the charioteer You have created me to be. So I'm coming up to You,
Lord. I'm heading into Your heavenly conveyance.

DAY 5
Deep Water

I called on the LORD in my distress. I cried to my God for help. He heard my
voice from his temple, and my cry for help reached his ears. . . . He spread
apart the heavens and came down with a dark cloud under his feet. He rode
on one of the angels as he flew, and he soared on the wings of the wind. . . .
He reached down from high above and took hold of me. He pulled me
out of the raging water. He rescued me from my strong enemy.
PSALM 18:6, 9–10, 16–17 GW

I'm in deep water, Lord. I never knew raising a child would bring so many
challenges. So I am crying out to You for help. Don't let me drown in these
waters filled with worldly woes. Reach down from on high and pull me out of
these tumultuous waves. Then quiet me and my ego with Your tender Word.
Give me a new vision where my spirit of service can blossom and grow.

Day 6
My Full Attention

O our God. . .we have no might to stand against this great company that is coming against us. We do not know what to do, but our eyes are upon You.
2 CHRONICLES 20:12 AMP

Sometimes I get so caught up in this world. But that is not where my victory lies. My hope, my saving grace, my true home, my triumph is in You, Lord. It doesn't matter if I don't have the answers today. There are no more ifs, ands, or buts. There is only You who knows and sees all. You have my full attention. No more worries. My eyes are on You and Your heavenly help.

Day 7
Because of You

Believe in the Lord your God and you shall be established; believe and remain steadfast to His prophets and you shall prosper.
2 CHRONICLES 20:20 AMP

You have opened the eyes of my heart, mind, body, spirit, and soul. The things of this world will soon enough fade away. That would sound a bit scary if I didn't know, if I didn't believe that You have promised to never leave me nor forsake me. So I'm counting all as lost except for knowing You and Your Son. Because of You, I prosper. Because of Your Word, I live.

CHAPTER 20
The Renewed Mother and Her Chosen Flight Plan

They cried out unto Him that loveth pilgrims, to make their way
more comfortable. So by that they had gone a little further, a wind arose,
that drove away the fog; so the air became more clear.
JOHN BUNYAN, *THE PILGRIM'S PROGRESS: PART 2*

• • • • • • •

*L*iving a life hidden in Christ has many facets and can be viewed in a variety of ways. One way to get to the heart of the matter in a unique and inspiring manner is to take a bird's-eye view of the human soul's yearning for flight. Doing so will help us to rise above the clouds of confusion to where the air is a little clearer.

As we considered the lilies in a previous chapter, Jesus asks us to look at the "birds of the air" (Matthew 6:26 NKJV). By looking to the birds, we find God not only has eyes on each and every sparrow but tells us we are of so much greater value to Him than they (see Luke 12:6–7). Jesus asks us to "consider the ravens, for they neither sow nor reap, which have neither storehouse nor barn; and God feeds them. Of how much more value are you than the birds?" (Luke 12:24 NKJV). King David wrote a song in which he first enumerates his woes and then says, "Oh, that I had wings like a dove! I would fly away and be at rest. Indeed, I would wander far off, and remain in the wilderness. I would hasten my escape from the windy storm and tempest" (Psalm 55:6–8 NKJV).

This plea, this innate desire for "wings," has been around as long as humankind has walked the face of this earth, the planet that was empty and dark until God's Spirit began "moving (hovering, brooding) over the face of the waters"

(Genesis 1:2 AMP). Since the very beginning of time, God, in creating us in His image, has made our souls to "mount up with wings," and nothing less than flying will truly satisfy them. Thus we are constantly seeking a way to fly from all that holds us down and hampers our rising up.

The problem is that we don't always recognize this fact that our way of escape is upward.

When we yearn to escape from life and its problems, to get beyond the mist and fog of confusion or grief from loss, we may attempt to "flee upon horses" (Isaiah 30:16 KJV), as the Israelites were wont to do when mired in mayhem. Horses are the outward things—some change of situation or help from our fellow man (or woman)—that we depend upon to relieve us. We saddle up and try to run north, south, east, or west, anywhere to escape our circumstances. But the only way to get clear of it all, the only way to find deliverance for our souls, is by mounting up with wings like eagles where the air is fresh and clear:

> *Those who wait for the Lord [who expect, look for, and hope in Him] shall change and renew their strength and power; they shall lift their wings and mount up [close to God] as eagles [mount up to the sun]; they shall run and not be weary, they shall walk and not faint or become tired. (Isaiah 40:31 AMP)*

But what are the wings we are to lift so that we can mount up to God? Their secret lies in the meaning of the words *those who wait for the Lord*. It means abiding in Him, hidden in Christ, surrendering ourselves to Him. It means trusting Him enough to rest in Him in that "secret place of the Most High" as Psalm 91:1 (AMP) says, for there we will "remain stable and fixed under the shadow of the Almighty [Whose power no foe can withstand]." Thus, our upward conveyance is found in our wings of perfect "trust" and complete "surrender." For only with these two wings will we be able to "mount up with wings as eagles" (Isaiah 40:31 KJV) to the "heavenly places" (Ephesians 2:6 KJV) in Christ Jesus, where worldly woes and frustrations will no longer have the power to disturb us. For the soul on wings overcomes the world by faith. Instead of being crushed by a mountainous obstacle, being wearied by attempting to go through it, or being put out of the way by having to go around it, the winged soul flies over the world and the things of it and in it. Such a soul is no longer *overcome by* but *comes over* those things that may tie or bind it to the earth. In this way, that spirit becomes more than a conqueror (see Romans 8:37). Smith writes:

> *Birds overcome the lower law of gravitation by the higher law of flight; and the soul on wings overcomes the lower law of sin and misery and bondage by the higher law of spiritual flying. The "law of the spirit of life in Christ Jesus" must necessarily be a higher and more dominant law than the law of sin and death; therefore the soul that has mounted into this upper region of the life in Christ cannot fail to conquer and triumph.*

So how is it that not all Christians find a consistent life of victory? The answer is that they do not "mount up with wings" into the higher life of Christ at all. Instead, they live on the same lowly plane as their circumstances. They try to fight them with earthly weapons. In doing so, they are overcome by worldly woes instead of becoming overcomers.

When we are riding above the storms of life, our eyesight becomes as sharp as our papa eagle's. Far above the world, we have keener perception and view things more clearly, for we are looking from a God-perspective. Our problems no longer look interminable or insurmountable or significant.

We need not cry out, "Oh, that I had wings, and then I would flee." For we already have our wings—trust and surrender. All we need to do is use them, mounting up on a constant and consistent basis so that our wings will build up their muscle! And then we can fly to God at any moment.

A mother eagle encourages her fledglings to fly by making their nest so uncomfortable that they are forced to leave it and take their chances in the unknown world beyond. Just so, God, our parent eagle, now "stirs up its nest" yet still "hovers over" us, "its young, spreading out its wings, taking them up, carrying them on its wings" (Deuteronomy 32:11 NKJV). God permits us to have troubles so that we don't get comfortable where we are but leave our own particular and personal comfort zones. Yet while we are in the midst of our ongoing transformations, as we become more and more like Christ, God continually cares for and protects us as we grow stronger and stronger. And when necessary, He will carry us until we are ready to soar where He wants us to soar.

We have been well fed as God, our eagle parent, has brought us the food of His Word, giving us new insights each time we look to Him for answers (see Psalm 63:7). Now we have grown to the point of soon being able to really try out our wings of trust and surrender. For if we have only one wing—trust *or* surrender—we never rise above the nest. We need to have and to use two wings—trust *and* surrender—to become airborne!

And, as mothers, we are not to just trust and surrender our own lives to God. We must trust and surrender the lives of our children as well. For we cannot mount up while holding our children in our arms—only our eagle Father God has the power to fly with fledglings in His embrace. Yes, we earthly mothers must trust our children to God and leave them—their struggles, their hardships, their situations, their ups and downs—fully in His capable hands. Thus unencumbered and unhindered, we can make our flight to God one of ultimate victory.

Tentatively at first, we follow our Master, first rising above our nests in brief test flights. The more we allow our souls to fly up out of ourselves, the more we are fueled with His courage and steeped in Christlikeness. Then suddenly we find ourselves leaving our comfort zones and taking flight. We've become full-fledged eagles!

Just as your child at one time ran to you as soon as he smelled trouble, the first place we will run to is God. He will not only lift us up out of trouble but will help us steer clear of the fowler's snare. But who exactly is this fowler (or perhaps more accurately, "fouler")? Who is it that fouls up our spiritual progress? It is the evil one who, like any other experienced fowler, sets his particular trap and bait depending on the type or condition of the bird he is seeking to ensnare.

Thus, there can be several hindrances to our airborne objectives. We can be imprisoned in a cage or net of sin; tethered to the ground by a cord of worldly woes;

weighted down with the heaviness of our emotions; or caught in any other snare of the fowler, which makes it impossible for the soul to rise up until the mighty power of God sets it free.

Mothers, do not let your wing of trust be weakened or disabled by sin and doubts. Also don't allow your wing of surrender to be weighted down by the heaviness of emotion or attachments to this world. Break every cord that hinders your upward progress. Trust and surrender all of *you*—and all of your children—to God's care.

Yet it's good to know that if, at times, we find ourselves too weak— emotionally, spiritually, physically, mentally—and we do not have the strength to fly, we can always look to God as our "place of refuge and a shelter from storm and from rain" (Isaiah 4:6 AMP). Amid life's tumults and tempests, all we need to do is pray, and God will either cover us in the shadow of His wings (see Psalm 57:1) or give us the strength we need to soar.

Which way do you choose? The path of happiness by trusting in and surrendering all to the Lord, allowing you to abide in Jesus, wait upon God, and soar above the storms, empowered by the Holy Spirit? Or the path of captivity to this world, tethered by ropes of discouragement, disappointment, wrongdoing, doubt, and fear?

If in accordance with God's wishes, we eagle mamas decide to break free from this world and rise up with Him, remember we can become airborne only when we do four things. The first is to *use our wings*, for we won't get one inch off the ground unless we do.

The second is to *not look to our emotions*. We cannot depend on them, for often they are false indicators of our spiritual reality. Instead, we rely solely on our wings of entire surrender to God and absolute trust in Him.

The third is to *not look to earthly solutions* to our problems. Instead, we are to set our "minds and keep them set on what is above (the higher things), not on the things that are on the earth" (Colossians 3:2 AMP). Like the Israelites, we are not to "flee upon horses" (Isaiah 30:16 KJV), because our enemies will have swifter ones and quickly catch up to us. Our best assurance is to look to God, who wants our eyes constantly upon Him and longs to rescue us from every earthly temptation, sin, sorrow, and trial (see Isaiah 30:18–20 AMP).

And the fourth and final is to *thank God for the blessings* we continually receive. Here, another lesson can be learned from our feathered friends:

> *One of the chickens went to the trough to drink, and every time she drank, she lifted up her head, and her eyes towards Heaven. See, said He [The Interpreter or Holy Spirit], what this little chick doth, and learn of her to acknowledge whence your mercies come, by receiving them with looking up. (John Bunyan,* The Pilgrim's Progress: Part 2*)*

Remember, we will be "more than conquerors" (see Romans 8:37 KJV) as we " 'seek those things which are above—not 'the things of the earth' because our lives are 'hid with Christ in God' " (Colossians 3:1–3 KJV).

> *For the promise is sure: "They that wait upon the Lord shall mount up with wings as eagles." Not "may perhaps mount up," but "shall." It is the inevitable result. May we each one prove it for ourselves!*
> HANNAH WHITALL SMITH

PATH MARKERS

Promise

Those who wait upon GOD get fresh strength. They spread their wings and soar like eagles, they run and don't get tired, they walk and don't lag behind.

ISAIAH 40:31 MSG

Proof

The LORD found Israel in a desert land. He found them in an empty and windy wasteland. He took care of them and kept them safe. He guarded them as he would guard his own eyes. He was like an eagle that stirs up its nest. It hovers over its little ones. It spreads out its wings to catch them. It carries them on its feathers. The LORD was the only one who led Israel. No other god was with them. The LORD made them ride on the highest places in the land.

DEUTERONOMY 32:10–13 NIrV

Provision

For He will give His angels charge concerning you, to guard you in all your ways. They will bear you up in their hands, that you do not strike your foot against a stone.

PSALM 91:11–12 NASB

Portrait

In Christ, I am raised up and sitting in heaven (see Ephesians 2:6).

Mind-Renewing Prayers

Day 1
Truly Home

*He who dwells in the secret place of the Most High
shall abide under the shadow of the Almighty. I will say of the* Lord,
"He is my refuge and my fortress; my God, in Him I will trust."
Psalm 91:1–2 nkjv

*There is no place better than being with You in my safe and secret place,
Lord. In You, I can escape all the demands of this world. In You, I am safe,
surrounded with a hedge of protection. In You I need never be afraid. In You, I
trust for all things. On this earth I am merely a pilgrim. Only in Your presence
do I feel as if I am truly home, needing nothing and no one but You.*

Day 2
Taking Cover

*Surely He shall deliver you from the snare of the fowler and
from the perilous pestilence. He shall cover you with His feathers,
and under His wings you shall take refuge. . . . You shall not be afraid.*
Psalm 91:3–5 nkjv

*There are so many ways I can be tripped up, Lord. But I'm counting on You
to keep me clear of the fouler. He seems to know all my weak points. So I'm
running to You, ready to take cover beneath Your massive wings. Here I am
safe. Here I need not be afraid.*

DAY 3

Supernatural Aid

*Praise the LORD, you angels, you mighty ones who carry out his plans,
listening for each of his commands. Yes, praise the LORD,
you armies of angels who serve him and do his will!*
PSALM 103:20–21 NLT

*Walking in the path You have laid out for me, I am never alone. You have
assigned angels to help me, to steer me clear of trouble. I am so glad You have
a plan for my life. Help me be as determined to follow You as You are to lead
me. Thank You, God, for all the supernatural aid you have bequeathed me. I
praise You, Your name, Your power, and Your love for me!*

DAY 4

The Ultimate Father

*"Because he has set his love upon Me, therefore I will deliver him; I will set him
on high, because he has known My name. He shall call upon Me, and I will
answer him; I will be with him in trouble; I will deliver him and honor him.
With long life I will satisfy him, and show him My salvation."*
PSALM 91:14–16 NKJV

*God, You know I love You with all my heart, spirit, soul, and mind. Because
of that You will deliver me. You will set me on high, above the cares and
callousness of this world. You will answer me when I cry out. For You are my
Abba God, the ultimate Father, doing the impossible, and working out all for
my good. Rescue me from this world and myself. I am hoping only in You.*

Day 5

God's Strength Rising

*This is what the Almighty L*ORD*, the Holy One of Israel, says:*
You can be saved by returning to me. You can have rest.
You can be strong by being quiet and by trusting me.
ISAIAH 30:15 GW

My soul longs to soar, Lord. Give me wings to fly high above this world and into Your presence. The only thing that saves me is returning and resting in You—because I have that privilege, and because You love it when I turn to You instead of attempting to "flee upon horses." In this moment, in this meditative silence, I feel Your strength rising within me.

Day 6

Catch My Breath

For He commands and raises the stormy wind, which lifts up the waves of the sea. . . . He calms the storm, so that its waves are still.
PSALM 107:25, 29 NKJV

I am always amazed at the miracles You perform—from the beginning of time to this very moment. You have so much at Your command. So, Lord, I'm counting on You to calm the wind and waves that are battering against me. Lift me up out of this flood. Take me to Your side, where I can catch my breath, lie in Your arms, and find the solace only You provide.

Day 7
Today and Forever

And He raised us up together with Him and made us sit down together
[giving us joint seating with Him] in the heavenly sphere
[by virtue of our being] in Christ Jesus (the Messiah, the Anointed One).
EPHESIANS 2:6 AMP

Hidden in Christ, I am seated in the heavenlies. There I feel Your presence and
see Your marvelous light. Thank You, Lord, for rescuing me from the darkness,
from the power of the fouler, and from the ways of this earthly existence. I'm
keeping my eyes on You and Your Son and putting all of myself—and my
children—in Your hands, today and forever.

CONCLUSION
The Pathway to Joy

*Tell them. . .of Christian, and Christiana his wife, and how she
and her children came after her husband. Tell them also
of what a happy end she made, and whither she is gone.*
JOHN BUNYAN, *THE PILGRIM'S PROGRESS: PART 2*

• • • • • • • •

*O*ur pathways to joy in the Lord are often straight with crooked lines. . . .

When Joy Tanchi Mendoza was fifteen years old, she was brutally raped by some men who broke into her home while her parents were out attending a Bible study. Joy writes, "At this point I met an important crossroad. A faith choice had to be made. Would I allow this tragedy to define my faith? Or, would I allow faith to define this tragedy?"

Joy and her family decided to hold on to the promise of Romans 8:28: "In all things God works for the good of those who love him" (NIV). In a later interview, Deonna Tanchi, Joy's mother, explained:

*The Bible says, "In everything, give thanks" [see 1 Thessalonians 5:18].
It sounds crazy. In a situation like that, how can you give thanks. I never
did say thank you that she's raped. But I said, "Lord, thank You for how
You're gonna use it." Thanking God is an act of surrender and faith.
And God put my heart at peace. . . . I had to hold on to that promise.
That hope that we have is the anchor for our soul [see Hebrews 6:19] no
matter what we go through, that hope in Him that He's gonna take care of
us and those we love as we hope in Him in His way and His time.*

This family's surrender and trust in God, in His love and His light, in His wisdom and His plan, turned harmful intentions into something good (see Genesis 50:20). Such was the beginning of their pathway from pain to healing. Joy is now married, has children of her own, and has a wonderful ministry in which she encourages others going through various trials. In her blog, she writes:

I want to encourage you by saying that God purposes to write each person's life story. The question is, will we let him hold the pen? It is his authorship that makes a life beautiful. When we fix our eyes on Jesus, "the author and perfector of our faith," we let him be the writer and the editor. (Hebrews 12:2) And, no matter how crooked or bent our way, no matter how laden with hardship the journey is, if it ends with God getting the glory, our tragedies turn into stories of God's grace to bless others and point them to Christ.

To Him Be the Glory!

The important thing for us is to know God loves us. He has a plan for our lives— and for the lives of our children. Although we may not be able to take away their pain, or our own, we can trust God as we go through it and so open up the highway to not only holiness and healing but happiness.

So cling to God's promises. Make them a part of your very life. Remain patient and trusting as you wait on the Lord. Continue to surrender yourself to Him and know that although He may be taking you the long way around, you *will* become the woman and mother He has created you to be and do the things on earth He has purposed you to do.

God never shuts a door without opening another. So do not be discouraged if you are not yet the woman you'd like to be or if you are not doing what you think God has meant you to do. Just be patient, surrender, trust, and know that your loving God is doing everything for your good. And that no matter what it looks like on the earthly plane, in the kingdom of God, all is well.

"All is well." In those three little words, we find the peace of God transcending and the joy of God unending. For there is nothing more profound than the encouraging and faithful spirit of the Shunammite mother who, when questioned by people in the midst of a crisis, as her son lay seemingly dead upon his bed, kept telling them that everything is and will be all right. (See chapter 9.)

We can take God's Word for that, for in *God Calling* we read:

> *My Keeping Power is never at fault, but only your realization of it. Not whether I can provide a shelter from the storm, but your failure to be sure of the security of that shelter.*
>
> *Every fear, every doubt, is a crime against My Love.*
>
> *Oh! children, trust. Practice daily, many times a day, saying, "All is well."*
>
> *Say it until you believe it, know it.*

To keep that spirit of certainty alive in you, try interspersing the words "All is well" into your daily breath and prayers. Take some time each day to sit before the Lord. Breathe deep. On the inhale, recite the words of the Lord's Prayer, lifting each phrase up to God as an offering. On the exhale, imagine God speaking directly to you as He repeatedly tells you that, no matter what the appearance, "all is well." Slowly and surely, firmly believing every word you offer to God and every word you receive back from Him, pray:

> *Our Father in heaven,*
> ALL IS WELL.
> *Hallowed be Your name.*
> ALL IS WELL.
> *Your kingdom come.*
> ALL IS WELL.
> *Your will be done*
> ALL IS WELL.
> *On earth as it is in heaven.*

ALL IS WELL.

Give us this day our daily bread.

ALL IS WELL.

And forgive us our debts,

ALL IS WELL.

As we forgive our debtors.

ALL IS WELL.

And do not lead us into temptation,

ALL IS WELL.

But deliver us from the evil one.

ALL IS WELL.

For Yours is the kingdom

ALL IS WELL.

and the power

ALL IS WELL.

and the glory forever.

ALL IS WELL.

Amen.

SO BE IT.

MATTHEW 6:9–13 NKJV

And while you are traveling down the pathway of happiness, following Christ as you walk in the Way, daily remind yourself who you are as a mother in Christ. Write your portrait attributes upon your heart so when feelings of dismay, fear, or discouragement threaten to overwhelm you and thoughts from the dark side begin to career around in your head, you may call these truths up, calm yourself, and bring light into not only your own life but also the lives of your children..

To help you see the full picture of who you truly are in Christ, your portrait's "features" are listed below. And if in your journey you find other attributes you'd like to add to this "sketch," please do so!

Each day, "put on the new self, which is being renewed in knowledge in the image of its Creator" (Colossians 3:10 TNIV) and allow your happiness in the Lord, which is strong and eternal, to overrule happenings. "Always be full of joy in the Lord. I say it again—rejoice!" (Philippians 4:4 NLT). And trust in the process of being complete in Christ:

> The LORD said to me. . ."If it seems slow in coming, wait patiently,
> for it will surely take place. It will not be delayed."
> HABAKKUK 2:2–3 NLT

Portrait

*I*n Christ. . .

I am able to have joy in any situation (see Philippians 4:4, 12).

I am being transformed into a new person (see 2 Corinthians 5:17).

I know God will provide me with everything I need (see Philippians 4:19).

I am standing firm (see 1 Thessalonians 3:8).

I am holy, pure in God's sight, and empowered by the Holy Spirit
(see Ephesians 1:4).

I live by faith, not by sight (see 2 Corinthians 5:7).

I have access to God's will (see 1 John 5:14).

I have access to God's direction and understanding (see 1 Corinthians 1:30).

I have inherited God's promises (see 2 Peter 1:3–4).

I am more than a conqueror (see Romans 8:37).

I am not only redeemed but forgiven (see Ephesians 1:7).

I am assured of God's presence in all situations (see Isaiah 43:2).

I am a freewoman, a daughter of God, and heir of His promises
(see Galatians 4:7).

I am growing in the grace and knowledge of the Lord (see 2 Peter 3:18).

I am strong enough to do whatever God calls me to do (see Philippians 4:13).

I am spiritually transformed with energy, strength, and purpose every day
(see Romans 12:1–2).

I am loved by God and delight to do His will (see John 14:21).

I am spiritually blessed because He lives in me (see Ephesians 1:3).

I am raised to new life, setting my eyes on the realities of heaven
(see Colossians 3:1).

I am raised up and sitting in heaven (see Ephesians 2:6).

*"Now I'm turning you over to God, our marvelous God whose gracious
Word can make you into what he wants you to be and give you
everything you could possibly need in this community of holy friends."*

Acts 20:32 msg

Note

1. Wikipedia defines *juggernaut* "in colloquial English usage. . .[as] a literal or metaphorical force regarded as mercilessly destructive and unstoppable. Originating ca. 1850, the term is a metaphorical reference to the Hindu Ratha Yatra temple car, which apocryphally was reputed to crush devotees under its wheels." *Merriam-Webster's Collegiate Dictionary,* 11th edition, defines *juggernaut* as "a large heavy truck" or "a massive inexorable force, campaign, movement, or object that crushes whatever is in its path."

About the Author

Donna K. Maltese is a freelance writer, an editor, and a writing coach, as well as a publicist for a local Mennonite project. Residing in Bucks County, Pennsylvania, with her husband and two adult children, Donna is active in her local church and enjoys serving with Mennonite Disaster Service.